Comments on other *Amazing Stories* from readers & reviewers

"Tightly written volumes filled with lots of wit and humour about famous and infamous Canadians."
Eric Shackleton, *The Globe and Mail*

"The heightened sense of drama and intrigue, combined with a good dose of human interest is what sets Amazing Stories *apart."*
Pamela Klaffke, *Calgary Herald*

"This is popular history as it should be... For this price, buy two and give one to a friend."
Terry Cook, a reader from Ottawa, on **Rebel Women**

"Glasner creates the moment of the explosion itself in graphic detail...she builds detail upon gruesome detail to create a convincingly authentic picture."
Peggy McKinnon, *The Sunday Herald*, on **The Halifax Explosion**

"It was wonderful...I found I could not put it down. I was sorry when it was completed."
Dorothy F. from Manitoba on **Marie-Anne Lagimodière**

"Stories are rich in description, and bristle with a clever, stylish realness."
Mark Weber, *Central Alberta Advisor*, on **Ghost Town Stories II**

"A compelling read. Bertin...has selected only the most intriguing tales, which she narrates with a wealth of detail."
Joyce Glasner, *New Brunswick Reader*, on **Strange Events**

"The resulting book is one readers will want to share with all the women in their lives."
Lynn Martel, *Rocky Mountain Outlook*, on **Women Explorers**

EXTREME CANADIAN WEATHER

EXTREME CANADIAN WEATHER

Freakish Storms and Unexpected Disasters

NATURE

by Joan Dixon

PUBLISHED BY ALTITUDE PUBLISHING CANADA LTD.
1500 Railway Avenue, Canmore, Alberta T1W 1P6
www.altitudepublishing.com
1-800-957-6888

Extreme care has been taken to ensure that all information presented in
this book is accurate and up to date. Neither the author nor the
publisher can be held responsible for any errors.

Publisher	Stephen Hutchings
Associate Publisher	Kara Turner
Series Editor	Jill Foran
Editor	Lori Burwash

We acknowledge the financial support of the Government
of Canada through the Book Publishing Industry Development
Program (BPIDP) for our publishing activities.

Altitude GreenTree Program
Altitude Publishing will plant twice as many trees as were used
in the manufacturing of this product.

We acknowledge the support of the Canada Council for the Arts which
in 2003 invested $21.7 million in writing and publishing throughout Canada.

 Canada Council   Conseil des Arts
for the Arts   du Canada

National Library of Canada Cataloguing in Publication Data

Dixon, Joan, 1957-
Extreme Canadian weather / Joan Dixon.

(Amazing stories)
Includes bibliographical references.
ISBN 1-55153-949-7

1. Natural disasters--Canada. I. Title. II. Series: Amazing stories (Canmore, Alta.)

QC941.D59 2004   363.34'92'0971   C2004-902703-4

An application for the trademark for Amazing Stories™
has been made and the registered trademark is pending.

Printed and bound in Canada by Friesens
2 4 6 8 9 7 5 3 1

To the heroes, and the survivors,
of Canada's strange weather.

Contents

Prologue 13

Chapter 1 Ice Storm 15

Chapter 2 Tornado Country 31

Chapter 3 The Dust Bowl. 43

Chapter 4 Blizzard of the Century 56

Chapter 5 Wreckhouse Winds 68

Chapter 6 Red River's Lakes 78

Chapter 7 Hurricanes — in Canada?. 95

Chapter 8 Hail Alley 112

Chapter 9 Firestorm 122

Epilogue 136

Bibliography 138

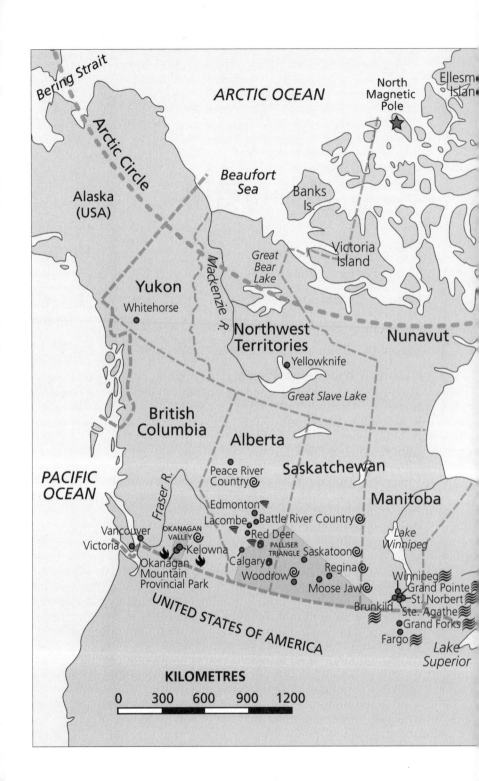

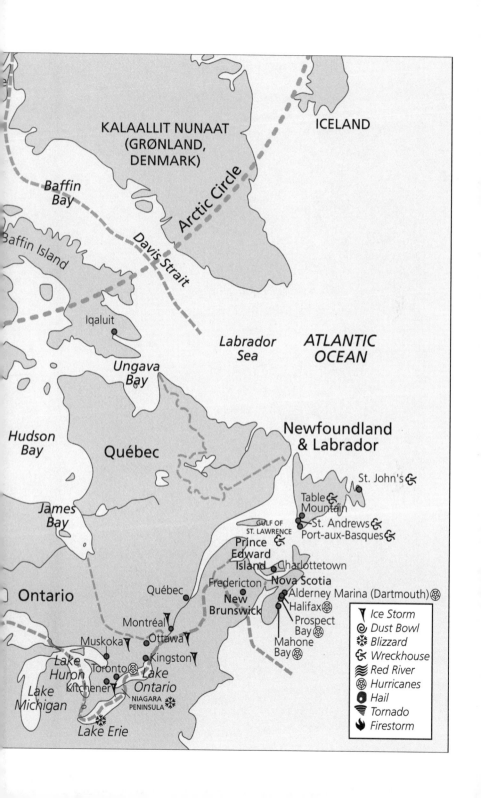

KALAALLIT NUNAAT
(GRØNLAND,
DENMARK)

ICELAND

Baffin
Bay

Arctic Circle

Baffin Island

Davis Strait

Iqaluit

Labrador
Sea

ATLANTIC
OCEAN

Ungava
Bay

Hudson
Bay

Québec

Newfoundland
& Labrador

St. John's ᚷ

James
Bay

Table ᚷ
Mountain

GULF OF
ST. LAWRENCE

St. Andrews ᚷ
Port-aux-Basques ᚷ

Prince
Edward
Island

Charlottetown

Ontario

Québec

Fredericton

New
Brunswick

Nova Scotia

Alderney Marina (Dartmouth) ⊛

Halifax ⊛

Prospect
Bay ⊛

Montréal

Muskoka

Ottawa

Mahone
Bay ⊛

Lake
Huron

Toronto

Kingston

Lake
Ontario

Lake
Michigan

Kitchener

NIAGARA
PENINSULA

Lake Erie

ⓨ	Ice Storm
☍	Dust Bowl
❄	Blizzard
ᚷ	Wreckhouse
≈	Red River
⊛	Hurricanes
◗	Hail
☗	Tornado
♨	Firestorm

Prologue

*Looking down onto her flooded street that night, 16-year-old
Sylvia Jones wished it was all just a terrible nightmare.*

*Clambering up behind her onto the roof of her house were
her father and several neighbours. Shivering and soaked to the
core from rain that had not stopped all week, they huddled
together, frightened and dazed in their bizarre circumstances.*

*Only a little earlier that evening, Sylvia and her father
had had to leave their stalled car in the middle of their street
and wade to the safety of their porch. Soon, not even the porch
was safe. The swollen Humber River had submerged it and
the ground floor so quickly, the roof became the only hope. If
Sylvia's father hadn't left a ladder up to it, they might already
have drowned, trapped inside their house.*

*When her parents built their new house on the flood
plain, they had anticipated a little flooding, but nothing like
this, and not in October. What they didn't know was that this
was no ordinary rainstorm.*

*As the refugees on the roof struggled to hang on in the
vicious winds, the force of the river ripped the house off its
foundations. Like an ark without a rudder, the house toppled
into the raging river.*

Sylvia shrieked. Through her flashlight's beam, she saw a

neighbour's house bobbing precariously in the current. Through the wind, she heard screams more desperate than her own.

As Sylvia watched and prayed, a volunteer firefighter in a small boat fought whitecaps to reach the neighbour's tipping house. Hands passed him a baby through the window. He made it as far as Sylvia's rooftop to hand her off before braving the treacherous waters to try to rescue the rest of the family.

Holding on to the baby as tightly as hope, Sylvia rocked her throughout that terrible night. The firefighter never returned. But at dawn's first light, other rescuers arrived. Gratefully, the exhausted teenager handed her young charge over, unaware that the baby was already an orphan. Her parents and brother had not survived the night — victims of Canada's 1954 hurricane, Hazel.

Chapter 1
Ice Storm

The year 1998 was one of epic weather disasters around the world: catastrophic hurricanes in the Caribbean, massive flooding in China and India, and droughts in Mexico and Central America. All were blamed on El Niño, a mysterious climatic event that happens every two to seven years. It means "the Christ child," so named by South American fishermen when they noticed it usually occurs at Christmastime. El Niño occurs when the buildup of warm water from the Pacific Ocean gets trapped off the western coast of South America, changing normal weather patterns globally.

For several years prior, Canadian government agencies, scientists, and insurance companies had been wondering publicly about the likelihood of major disasters in Canada as a result of El Niño. Many worst-case scenarios were described, including floods and earthquakes. None included the possibility of an ice storm that could paralyze Quebec.

The freakish event happened in January 1998, when a huge warm, wet air mass from the Gulf of Mexico collided with stationary heavy, cold air from the Arctic. Unable to push the cold air off, the layers of warm air sandwiched themselves between the cold layers. A thick layer of cold air would have produced snow, but the thin layer allowed raindrops to form in the warm air above and fall through to the cold air below.

Freezing rain doesn't usually last long because the conditions must be "just so." Only when the temperature hovers around the freezing mark can clouds vacillate between liquid or frozen precipitation. But a lingering large high-pressure system blocked the Gulf storms from following their normal track out toward the Atlantic.

Winter Wonderland

Even by Montreal standards, the first winter storm of 1998 was a doozy. As discarded Christmas trees waited on the curb for pickup along with the rest of the holiday trash, morning newscasters reported that a warm front approaching from the southwest had stalled east of Montreal.

The night before, January 4, had turned cold, and throughout the night, the precipitation had been a confusing mix. What started as snowflakes soon turned into cold raindrops. When the rain hit the ground, it spread out and froze, forming a thin veneer of ice over everything.

When Montrealers woke up on Monday, they were greeted by a dull, grey, overcast morning — and a world of ice. Everything was covered with a crystallizing coating of water. The unearthly scenes lured photographers outside, worried the ice sculptures might soon melt.

But the warm front normally expected after freezing rain did not arrive. Within hours, the beauty of the silvery ice began to turn lethal. One long-time easterner said, "It was the strangest thing I have experienced in all my years ... This was not fairy tale–like, this was frightening. It was frightening because it was coming down and down and down and it didn't stop."

The infamous jet stream was holding the weather pattern in place. The first day dropped 20 millimetres of freezing rain. Trees were the first casualty. Roots ripped from the ground, millions of trees fell all over Montreal.

Living on the worst-hit West Island, Pamela Patchet Hamilton and her husband were awakened during the night by an enormous crash on the roof that shook the whole house. A tree in their backyard had fallen, taking out the cable, phone line, and mast holding the hydro line to the house before settling on the back porch.

Pamela recalled the sounds that began her ordeal: "At first the rain thrummed against the windows. As the ice formed on the trees, the icy branches clacked together then broke under the weight of the ice with huge cracks. The branches literally exploded under all the weight, and huge trees snapped in half with thunderous cracks at random intervals. They sounded like loud gunshots."

After the trees, the next casualties were utility poles. As the freezing rain continued to fall, ice caked up on the power lines. Vibrating wildly in the wind, thousands of poles fell like the trees. Normally, snapped power lines and even poles could be quickly repaired once the rain stopped. This time, however, the huge power pylons — 130 major transmission towers built to withstand only 15 millimetres of freezing rain — crumpled as well.

The blackouts started Monday afternoon. In one packed movie theatre, the season's most popular film, *Titanic*, stopped coincidentally at the part when the doomed ship lost its own power. Even the Outremont home of the premier of Quebec, Lucien Bouchard, was not spared the power outage. To oversee the deteriorating situation, he delayed his trip to Latin America, telling reporters he expected to join the Team Canada economic mission shortly.

Paralyzed City

On Tuesday, the second day of freezing rain, schools and offices in Montreal and the surrounding area were forced to close. The entire downtown and west end were in the dark — no lights in the buildings, no streetlights, and in many cases, no heat. People were told to stay home unless it was an

Ice Storm

A woman walks past a downed hydro pylon near
St-Constant, Quebec. January 15, 1998.

emergency. Broken electrical wires still arced colourful deadly sparks and made going anywhere dangerous. Residential
streets were slippery and blocked by ice-encrusted branches
or trees. Cars were smashed by fallen trees. Many highways
were not negotiable — getting anywhere in Montreal, or leaving it, was nearly impossible.

Power outages were sporadic but spreading. Falling
wires touching each other, or too much demand, threatened
to shut down the power grid entirely. As long as the freezing

rain kept falling, repair crews knew there was no point restoring lines. Hospitals lost their primary power; traffic lights went out. With no power, TV and radio stations were unable to broadcast. Some areas would have power restored only to lose it again a little while later.

After a few days, the whole of the West Island was not only coated in ice and darkness, it was amazingly quiet. No hum of appliances or traffic noise. In the meantime, the Hamilton family listened to its battery-powered radio and used the fireplace to heat and cook. Seven hundred thousand other Montrealers did the same.

A rash of fires resulted from using alternative heating methods. The storm claimed its first victim, 82-year-old Rolland Parent, who died of accidental carbon monoxide poisoning. He had been trying to stay warm by running a generator in his basement. In another Montreal home, an electrical fire broke out, trapping a two-year-old. Fortunately, a firefighter managed to rescue the child. The next day, however, the storm claimed another victim. More than 5000 other people called 911.

The Longest Train Ride

The freezing rain didn't stop, and at least 35 more millimetres were expected on Wednesday, with no spells of sunshine or thaw between downpours. The ice layers grew thicker.

That day, Ottawa was also hit. The ice rain coated Parliamentary statues and left the prime minister's house in the dark. Jean Chrétien was forced to delay his trip to Latin America as well.

Other more local trips departed optimistically. A VIA train left Ottawa for Toronto on schedule, but 45 minutes into the ride, broken trees blocked the track. Commuters were told only that they might experience delays. No one complained much at first, but when the train ran out of food after an hour — on a normally 4-hour trip — the mood changed.

After 7 or 8 more hours, passengers became resentful, unaware of the magnitude or scope of the weather crisis affecting the train. Tempers flared. When VIA Rail would not estimate the delay or provide an emergency procedure plan, a group of passengers took over, divvying up any available food, water, cell phones, and first-class perks.

After about 13 hours, the train finally reached Kingston. The empowering spirit of cooperation ensured the rest of the extraordinary 18-hour "train ride from hell," in the words of one passenger, became one of camaraderie. By Thursday, Via Rail knew to cancel eastbound trains from Toronto. Airlines also cancelled flights.

Adventures in Coping

Freezing rain immobilized more of Ontario — reaching as far north as Muskoka and as far west as Kitchener — before moving east to New Brunswick and Nova Scotia and south to New York State and New England. In the triangle of darkness centred around Montreal, more freezing rain fell. A million homes were without power.

Some people fared better than others. For the first day or so, as in any adventure, the trials provided a novel challenge. The crisis brought people together, and neighbourhoods became neighbourly. People without power hopscotched from one house to the next as rotating blackouts affected areas randomly.

Anyone who was lucky enough to have power found themselves sharing. It was not unusual to see more than a dozen extras at the supper table as neighbours opened their homes and families moved in with extended families. Everyone assumed their hospitality would be needed for a short time only. One family bravely hosted nine neighbourhood boys, who treated the event like a summer camp and didn't want to go home.

In the beginning, the challenges seemed surmountable for those who had lived through short times without power and heat. Newcomers to the country, however, weren't sure they were going to survive. One student from Fiji, isolated and huddled under blankets in his apartment, worried about how he was going to cope with what he could only assume was a "normal" winter.

Outside the city, rural dwellers were dealing with a situation that was even more dangerous. More than 274,000 cows were at risk on the 23,000 farms affected. Many didn't survive. David Fraser, whose family operated three dairy farms, suffered little disruption thanks to a generator. He shared his good fortune with neighbours who weren't so well equipped. Desperate farmers would wake up at 2:00 a.m. for their turn with his generator.

Not everyone was as good-hearted or community-minded in this crisis. A bomb threat forced the evacuation of one shelter. The kilometre-long lineups at gas stations induced tense outbreaks. There were reports of looting and thefts, especially of scarce generators, which had to be guarded or locked up, or they would be resold at black market prices. The police braced for stress-induced anarchy.

Help Required

Finally, on January 8, after an uncomfortable 72 hours without a break in the bizarre weather, Premier Bouchard recognized that he had to declare a state of emergency. The potential for loss of life was increasing. The separatist leader reluctantly appealed to the federal government to send in help.

The 12,000 troops (and 4000 more in Ontario) of Operation Recuperation represented the largest humanitarian assistance of the Canadian Forces to date. Although they had not been seen on the streets of Montreal since the 1970 October Crisis, troops were now welcomed with open arms.

Experienced with helping in weather crises — most recently the big flood in Manitoba the year before — the troops set up emergency shelters, evacuated those in need, delivered supplies, shovelled snow and ice, and helped hydro crews. They tried to manage the chaos by restoring calm and hope.

Despite everyone's herculean efforts, things got worse. The fifth day, Friday, January 9, brought even more freezing rain, making it the storm's worst and fiercest — 100 millimetres had fallen in some places by the end of the week. Transportation was impossible: even the underground subway system, the Metro, was shut down. Another worry and danger of the extended crisis was the shortage of clean water. The filtration system was crippled without power, and its reserves were running out.

Fortunately, hydro workers came in from Manitoba, the Maritimes, and the U.S. to help restore emergency power. One worker from New Jersey commented that the ice storm's effect seemed worse than a hurricane's. Thunder and lightning late on "Dark Friday" added to the chaos, but signalled a much-needed change of weather — after about 90 hours of freezing rain.

The change was too late for the hydro-electric system, which was on the brink of collapse. Four of the five links of the "ring of power" feeding Montreal had failed. As climatologist David Phillips noted, this was a system that had taken half a century to build but was knocked down by nature in mere hours.

Half Quebec's population — 1.4 million homes and businesses — was without power. Hydro-Québec had no contingency plan, no crisis management department, not even a computer simulation of this potential emergency scenario.

Riding Out the Storm

One out of every four Quebeckers had to seek refuge with friends or family at some point during the storm. The hardest part was that they couldn't do anything to make the power come back any sooner. They couldn't even escape. Transportation in and out of the area was virtually impossible. Two million people were trapped on the island of Montreal and they didn't know for how long.

Long-term survival strategies kicked into gear. Hundreds of shelters set up anywhere there was power and space — office buildings, shopping malls, hockey arenas. Some were more comfortable and welcoming than others. Even the best ones quickly became dreary places to spend day and night while people worried about what they would have to deal with later. After experiencing the long lineups for showers, one woman said she would never take hot water and clean towels for granted again.

For those who stayed at home, everyday life became an ordeal after the first few days. The same storm a hundred years ago might not have been such a crisis. Not only were electric fridges, stoves, and furnaces useless, but also the sump pumps needed to deal with floods resulting from burst frozen pipes. One resident who was advised to boil water almost laughed — how was she supposed to do that when she didn't have power? Gas and wood stoves became invaluable. A radio show explained how to cook on a car's exhaust manifold — that is, if people had any gas.

For the Hamilton family, accustomed to camping, it was a brief return to the past. In addition to chopping firewood and tending the fire, the kids pulled out board games and cards, told stories or read books aloud by candlelight, and played charades for amusement.

Fatal Weather

For other people, the storm was more than just an ordeal to get through — it presented real dangers ... and sometimes even tragedies. One exhausted emergency worker came home to a warning smell. She located a kerosene lamp her family and guests had been using — just as it was ready to explode. A volunteer firefighter had to do the unthinkable. She requested Hydro-Québec to turn *off* the power to a house that had recently regained its precious service after a minor fire.

After the first week of endless rain and temperatures hovering around the freezing point, the precipitation had stopped, but the weather turned much colder. Police rescued a group of 39 elderly people huddled together in one residence lacking heat or electricity.

Not everyone was as lucky. All told, the ice storm and its aftermath were responsible for at least 35 deaths — 22 in Quebec and 13 elsewhere. People died falling off roofs they were trying to de-ice to save their houses from collapse. They also died of hypothermia, heart attacks, or carbon monoxide poisoning; they were crushed by ice or fatally burned while trying to stay warm. Livestock and pets suffered and perished, too. Fish were frozen in suspended animation in their icy aquariums. Other people came close. A man had to stitch himself up when he sliced his leg open cutting firewood, then almost froze to death later. Many others suffered frostbite, burns, and scratched corneas from chipping ice. Pneumonia was not uncommon either, and so many people moving to shelters caused a serious outbreak of flu, taxing the already overwhelmed hospitals.

Seeing the Light
While some people suffered stress and depression as the crisis worsened, others turned the crisis into a mission. Volunteering and sharing their resources kept them from complaining or going crazy. The Red Cross mobilized 3300 staff and volunteers to help throughout the emergency. Hundreds of volunteer firewood choppers from other provinces filled the desperate need to keep fires burning.

By day 9 of the Hamiltons' blackout, the roads around their home were finally cleared, so Pamela decided to treat the kids to a hot breakfast at a McDonald's that had power. "None of us had showered and we were at the end of our collective ropes. We straggled into McD's, standing at the counter, smelling of wood smoke and worse. I started to order when the kid behind the counter interrupted me. 'I'm sorry, ma'am, but it's 10:31. We stop serving breakfast at 10:30.'" She looked at him in disbelief. "'Isn't there anything you can do? We've been without power for nine days.' 'Sorry. Company policy,' he shrugged." The tension that had been building since the ice storm hit Pamela all at once. Howling out of control, her head thrown back, she couldn't stop the flood of tears. Mortified, her three young children tried to move her outside. Calming a little, they eventually drove to another establishment. "An angel in the form of a waitress took one look at me and gently guided me to a table," Pamela recalled gratefully. "She appeared in an instant with a newspaper and a hot cup of coffee. It was as soothing and soul-satisfying as a mother's hug."

It wasn't until day 13 that the family had power restored. A family friend had delivered a hot homemade turkey dinner, complete with soup, gravy, stuffing, and apple pie. Within a few hours of their morale-boosting dinner, the power suddenly came on. "Lights blared and we shielded our eyes, unused to the brightness after almost two weeks of candlelight," Pamela recounted. The crisis was over, and the McDonald's Breakfast Breakdown is now a humorous part of Hamilton family lore.

Returning to Normal

After two weeks, power was gradually restored in Montreal. In some areas, it took as long as 33 days. Power consumption was lower after the storm for a while, indicating perhaps a new respect for electricity. One returned evacuee wondered if anything else would be the same again. But spring seed catalogues soon arrived with the mail carriers, who were finally back on the job.

By January 21, the weather was back to normal, −11°C and sunny, and so was the morning rush hour, even though 150,000 people were still without power. Kids were keen to go back to school, and their parents were gradually shaking off the residue of trauma. Long lines were expected as the first cheques for power outage were issued to Montrealers — 10 "Bouchard Bucks" per day per person for each day without electricity — not a windfall, but some unexpected compensation.

More than a month later, ice remained on the sidewalks of Montreal, in spite of the work of jackhammers and ice picks. The cold weather had welded the ice, and later snow, to the ground. Travel was still treacherous, but most of the 100,000 evacuees were back home. All but 65,000 had their power restored.

The storm became Canada's most expensive natural disaster — resulting in $3 billion in damages. However, no dollar figure could be placed on the fear, losses, and inconvenience of the ice storm. And "nobody could repair a broken tree." Arbourists did try, but an estimated 25 percent of Montreal's trees were lost. The effect of the ice storm on the maple syrup industry was considered irreversible.

Since the storm, Hydro-Québec has improved its disaster response and bolstered its transmission system with new pylons and stronger cables. Many residents of the triangle of darkness, acknowledging their vulnerability, have improved their preparation, too — stocking up on generators, candles, and wood stoves in case of a repeat. This ice storm had tested even the hardiest of Canadians accustomed to the country's extreme winter weather.

Chapter 2
Tornado Country

Tornadoes may seem like an unlikely weather phenomenon in Canada, but the deadly "twisters" most often associated with the American Midwest are more common than people think. Environment Canada documents up to 80 tornadoes touching down across the country each year — about 5 percent of the world's total, and second most after the United States. Hundreds more may go unnoticed and unreported because they hit unpopulated areas and do little damage.

Most reported tornadoes touch down in bands across British Columbia, the Prairie provinces, Ontario, Quebec, and New Brunswick. The Canadian end of North America's Tornado Alley, in southwestern Ontario, may get more frequent tornadoes than Alberta, but usually none bigger. Two of Alberta's most recent tornadoes rate in Canada's list of top five worst. Tornadoes are rated in severity from F1 to F5. Officially at least, Canada has never been hit with an F5. But tornadoes can strike without warning and move quickly — most last less than 15 minutes, some only seconds. They're hard to predict, and their devastation can be horrific and long lasting.

In July 1987, the deadliest twister in Alberta — an F4 — hit the Evergreen trailer park near Edmonton. Lasting an incredible 50 minutes on the ground, it left a wake of destruction 40 kilometres long. The tornado killed 27 people, hospitalized 53, and injured 250. The severe weather warnings preceding it were either inadequate because they were late or, as often is the case, not heeded. Following the disaster, a report recommended that campgrounds be equipped with special weather radios.

Camping Weekend

Pine Lake is a peaceful 7-kilometre-long lake set in a bowl surrounded by rolling, forested hills near Red Deer, Alberta. Campgrounds, cabins, and farms rim the spring-fed lake, normally a quiet haven for boating, fishing, and other recreation. Pine Lake also happens to be located in the central Alberta storm track — an area known for severe tornadoes.

Thirteen years after the Evergreen tornado, on July 14, 2000, campers were starting to arrive for the weekend at Pine Lake. More than 1000 people were expected at one of its largest campgrounds, idyllically named Green Acres.

The weather for the weekend looked promising. The temperature during the day had hit 30°C. The sky had been clear and the early evening was still warm and muggy. There was no hint that anyone would have to change their plans due to severe weather.

At the start of the third week of Jim Knudson's family vacation, this day had been the highlight. They'd spent the day in a rental boat and were looking forward to an evening swim and treat of ice cream at the Green Acres Campground store.

As they were preparing dinner in their trailer, Jim checked the local TV news. Meteorologists were predicting only the possibility of thunderstorms for the Red Deer area, 60 kilometres northwest. This was normal for hot summer days in the region, so he didn't worry. From his location deep in the low-lying campground, he could see only hints of clouds coming over the surrounding hills.

Tracking the Storm
The summer of 2000 had been a busy one for meteorologists at Environment Canada's Prairie Storm Prediction Centre in Winnipeg. They had already tracked at least 685 severe weather events, including 91 tornadoes (the average is 43) and 130 funnel clouds. Despite their sophisticated resources, meteorologists can only watch for conditions favourable for the development of a supercell thunderstorm — the largest and most dangerous type of storm found in the prairies — and guess the broad general area it might affect.

This particular day, forecasters were working on more than a hundred severe weather bulletins and nine tornado warnings in the prairies. They had also been tracking a potential supercell thunderstorm shortly after it formed at 3:30 p.m. over the foothills of the Rocky Mountains. Around 4:30 p.m., the radar showed large thunderclouds being pushed by the strong winds that cruise along the tops of the mountains east toward central Alberta.

At 5:30 p.m., the storm grew larger when it collided with a belt of moist, warm air. A well-developed southern edge to the cloud formation was clearly visible to people around Red Deer and Lacombe. A few minutes later, Environment Canada meteorologists released a severe thunderstorm watch — they knew now it was a supercell capable of producing a severe storm, but couldn't specify where, or even if, it would spawn anything worse.

An off-duty meteorologist who happened to be near Red Deer at the time phoned in to report the storm's cloud base lowering rapidly around 6:00 p.m. Weather watchers know these are ominous signs. Hail the size of golf balls began to fall in Red Deer, breaking car windows.

Unaware of the change in weather report, most Pine Lake campers continued to go about preparing supper. Despite the 1987 recommendation, there were no special weather radios to tell them that at 6:18 p.m. a thunderstorm watch had been upgraded to a severe thunderstorm *warning* that was specific to their area and included the possibility of high winds, heavy rain, and hailstones. It also carried the reminder that tornadoes could form in a severe thunderstorm. Only 1 in 10 supercell thunderstorms will create a tornado. What the warning couldn't say was whether this might be the one.

The storm that was born out of the clash of two weather fronts was already causing severe thunderstorms that moved across Alberta. At 6:40 p.m., the pilots who had been seeding clouds to suppress potential hail were called off. According to their moisture-monitoring radar, the storm was growing far too quickly for the hail-busters to do any good.

It was getting dangerous, too. When the clouds met a band of low-level moisture just west of Pine Lake, the conditions for a vortex of wind 300 km/h were created.

Shortly before 7:00 p.m., huge black clouds — topped by the distinctive anvil shape unique to thunderstorms — appeared over the edge of the hills around the sheltered Pine Lake. With almost no warning, heavy rain and hail the size of oranges began to fall.

In the campground, Jim Knudson and Kelly Garrett rushed around taking awnings down and putting away their respective families' belongings. Jim's TV screen turned dark as the power cut off. Taking shelter in her trailer, Kelly lay on top of her frightened children to protect them from the deafening noise of the hailstones and the shaking of the wind. All of a sudden, they heard a big explosion as the trailer next to them landed on their slide-out.

Tornado!

A tornado warning can be issued only when an eyewitness sees a tornado touch down. Still, many people would not have recognized the tornado for what it was. It looked more like a massive grey wall than the typical cone-shaped funnel. By 7:00 p.m., a tornado had in fact already touched down 8 kilometres west of the lake and was racing toward Green Acres Campground. Just before the tornado struck the campground's southwest edge, the sky turned black and the wind increased to 300 km/h, screaming like a multitude of jet engines.

Then all hell broke loose.

There was nowhere to hide from the tornado. Several campers, including 75-year-old Phyllis Gelleberg, who had spent 15 summers at Pine Lake without experiencing weather like this, headed for the shelter of their cars. The back windows of one truck smashed in over its occupants while the driver sat with eyes closed and her foot on the brake in a futile effort to keep the vehicle stationary, praying like she "never had prayed before."

Jim's eight-year-old daughter screamed as she looked outside their trailer to see the one next door stand up on its back end and tip over. The family felt their own trailer lift up and hit a tree next to where they had parked. The extreme wind shook the trailer continuously for four long minutes. Mangled trees and trailers flew past their windows.

The tornado's explosive force snapped trees and flipped

other trailers and cars three storeys high into the air. It lifted mobile homes from their pads and wrapped skeletal frames around tree trunks. A large part of one house's roof was torn from its frame, and the cinder block laundry facility was demolished. The wind flung debris into huge piles or tossed it haphazardly across the open ground.

No shelter was safe. Phyllis was plucked from her car and hurled headlong through the air. Six-year-old Devon Kline was hiding in terror under the slide in the playground. A tree branch flying through the air hit him, rupturing his spleen. The tornado didn't give two-year-old Lucas Holtom a chance — tearing him right out of his father's arms.

After the tornado ripped through the campground, it crossed the lake, overturning boats and knocking down a stand of trees on a narrow peninsula. Then it flattened one cabin.

At another cabin on the lake's east shore, Dave Lauzon and friends had been enjoying hamburgers and beer when he noticed the sudden blackness outside. They rushed to put blankets on their cars, but the hail's rough sting quickly drove them back in. The screen door was ripped from Dave's hands and it took three people to close the main door. Dave could see his friend's lips moving but couldn't hear what he was screaming. He saw a tree fall on one of the cars.

A wall of white replaced the lake. Fish were sucked out of the water and spewed all over the beach, while trailers and vehicles were sucked *into* the lake. Dave and his friends tried to escape their cabin for another one with a basement but were blocked by falling trees. Retreating, they hoped for the best and huddled in their cabin on stilts.

The tornado moved east for 10 more minutes before it died. It demolished crops and rearranged livestock on farms. The thunderstorm itself crossed over into Saskatchewan and dissipated shortly after midnight.

Because of its power and devastation, the Pine Lake tornado was rated a minimum of F3 — a moderate to severe disaster. The people at Pine Lake couldn't imagine anything worse.

Devastation

After the tornado crossed the lake, a momentary calm descended over the campground. In the distance far to the east, flashes of lightning preceded the rumbling of thunder. The wind died down, and the rain and hail stopped. The sun even came out, as it generally does after a thunderstorm passes. The evening was calm and gorgeous.

Then, at 7:05 p.m., the exact time a tornado warning was finally issued, the RCMP began receiving calls for help. One of the first callers told the 911 dispatcher that her husband had hurt his elbow. In her panic, she forgot to mention the tornado.

Immediately after the tornado, campers had rallied and formed into groups to help one another. Even a man who had just lost his mother worked frantically to help others before emergency workers could arrive from outside.

The fire chief of Red Deer County, Cliff Fuller, was the first on the scene. He served as incident commander for the rescue effort. As he drove toward the campground on the road above it, he saw huge uprooted trees, stacks of hay bales, and granaries knocked to the ground.

Over its entire path of 24.5 kilometres, the Pine Lake tornado had followed a distinct line and scattered debris outward in all directions. The path widened from 50 metres to 1.6 kilometres. At its heart lay a 250-metre-wide swath of total destruction, covering 400 campsites.

Cliff knew he was coming into something very bad. The campground appeared as if a wall had separated its two sections. On the north edge of the tornado's path, the campground lay practically untouched. A few trailers and motor homes had been pushed over, but the damage was limited.

The southern half was devastated — the scene resembled a war zone. Jagged tree trunks pointed skyward like bare fence posts, trailers impaled on some. One trailer had a picnic table embedded in its side. Another was sitting almost 2 metres off the ground on a tree.

Disheveled, distraught people were leaving the campground. In obvious shock, one man was walking along the road looking for his father and two kids. They had left him only two minutes before the tornado hit, and he had no idea where they were.

Throughout the campground's southern half, the tornado seemed to have randomly chosen what it destroyed. On one site, a trailer had been ripped apart, while on the site next to it, a tent trailer was intact. Amid chaos and debris, rescuers came across a picnic table still set for two people, complete with wineglasses and a tablecloth. A pot of peas sat untouched.

Search and Recovery

Cliff sent his crew down the hill to begin helping survivors. He established his command post at the top of the hill, where cell phone reception was possible. Throughout the evening, fire and rescue crews kept arriving — some from as far away as Calgary and Edmonton.

A triage area was established in the playground. Blood and stretchers were everywhere. A large group of walking wounded sat on a nearby hill, waiting for evacuation to a community centre. Other people refused to leave, worried about missing friends or relatives. Some had last been seen walking by the beach just before the storm.

By nightfall, only 300 of the 1000 campers had been accounted for. Turning on bright searchlights, rescuers kept searching through the mangled metal and wood that looked like a bomb's aftermath. Despite the ambulances and helicopters, the site was strangely quiet.

As emergency workers covered another seemingly lifeless body with a blanket, they added Phyllis Gelleberg to the list of tornado victims. Fortunately, before her bloody and battered body could slip into the coma that would last two weeks, a campground employee heard her crying. She was transported to hospital with more than a hundred others. Seven bodies were found during the initial search. Later, one more was recovered. Scuba divers from the Calgary Fire Department were brought in to search for bodies in the vehicles submerged in the lake. Much to the rescuers' relief, they found no other victims. At 4:30 a.m., Cliff had to call off the search when the weather turned bad. But at 6:00 a.m., when the sun came up, rescue teams started combing the wreckage again for survivors or bodies. They still didn't know who or what they were looking for. It would be 10 days before the search and recovery was complete.

Lasting Memories

Environment Canada calculates the odds of being killed by a tornado as 12 million to 1. Of the 130 people who were sent to hospital, 4 died, bringing the total dead to 12. At least half of the hospitalized had suffered potentially life-threatening injuries.

For months after, little Devon Kline was scared to wander outdoors and headed inside if the leaves so much as rustled. For Phyllis, who lost a leg and an elbow and acquired numerous physical scars, it was exactly two years to the day before she was well enough to leave the hospital and consider going near Pine Lake again. Some survivors say they will never return.

The first killer twister in 13 years, the 2000 Pine Lake

tornado was not the last in Alberta. Almost exactly one year later, a tornado touched down in a field not far from Pine Lake. Another in 2004 came closer. Although neither did much damage, they reminded people in tornado country to pay attention to weather warnings.

In the aftermath of the Pine Lake tornado, Dave Lauzon had to clean up the debris transported over from the other side of the lake. Among the items, he found golf balls and a life jacket from Green Acres campground. He kept a golf ball — his own reminder of how lucky he was to be spared that tragic day.

Chapter 3
The Dust Bowl

Since the settlement of the prairies, weather has been farmers' greatest challenge — in the form of persistent and unpredictable droughts. These prolonged shortages of water are the result of a lack of precipitation, hot dry air, low soil moisture — or all three.

Drought can occur in every type of climate, but the semi-arid southern prairie is particularly vulnerable since its precipitation is so variable. Any rain the area receives comes from the west, but the wind sweeping east from the Pacific leaves much of its moisture over the mountains. By the time the wind reaches the area, it is often hot — and dry.

Perhaps nowhere else in Canada are people more weather-obsessed, or weather-dependent, than in the prairies.

They have learned the hard way that droughts can beget other droughts, and bring disaster.

Settling the Dry West

The prairie lands were not suitable for farming or settlement — this was the warning Captain John Palliser, leader of one of Canada's earliest scientific expeditions, gave the governments of Britain and Canada in 1863. The most arid region of central and southern Alberta, Manitoba, and much of southern Saskatchewan — later called the Palliser Triangle — was especially unsuitable for growing crops because it had a dry climate, sandy soil, and extensive grass cover. Cactuses even grew along the coulee ridge.

In 1870, Dominion government botanist John Macoun disputed Palliser's observations. Macoun believed the prairies were a lush landscape well suited for agriculture. The reason they disagreed was simple — Macoun experienced the prairies during a wet year and Palliser saw the area during a dry year.

Choosing to follow Macoun's advice, the Canadian Pacific Railway moved its proposed rail line south into the dry prairies. And the Canadian government either forgot or ignored Palliser's warnings and prepared to populate the west.

By 1910, one-quarter of Canada's population lived in the west. Drawn to the area's sandier soil, which was easier to clear, settlers farmed as they had in their homelands in eastern Canada and Europe. Their techniques, ideas, and technology were better suited to those wetter, more humid climates.

But this was an area subject to drought, and newcomers had much to learn about its peculiarities. For instance, to reach maturity, wheat — the region's main crop — needed 28 to 33 centimetres of rain from spring until harvest. Five centimetres less could wither a crop. There were sturdier crops better suited to prairie summers, but most farmers had yet to discover this or the techniques that could have helped them endure more successfully the unforgiving prairie weather.

The Dust Bowl Fills

The early years of settlement were dry. Every family seemed to have a similar story. Like many other immigrants, Ken Scheffelmaier's great-grandfather and grandfather had left a different kind of hardship in Russia to begin anew in Canada. Droughts that followed forced them from their original destination near Hanna, Alberta, northward to try again in Battle River country.

Son of an Ontario farmer, Howard Lawrence moved west as a young man to homestead near Woodrow, in south-central Saskatchewan. "Dad was always determined to be a first-class farmer," his daughter, Juanita Ruse, said. Despite this determination, Howard was often forced to move on in a different way, taking on other work to support his dream.

After the initial dry years, the weather cooperated to produce a series of good crops. The summer of 1928 was an especially good one for prairie farmers. Their record wheat harvest earned a reasonable price. Both the

Scheffelmaier and Lawrence families teemed with optimism and went into 1929 thinking the good years would continue.

That spring, however, searing winds and modest rain kept their harvest small. The Scheffelmaiers discovered they had moved just in time for even greater hardship.

On October 29, 1929, the stock market collapsed and the world economy crumbled, along with the price and market for wheat, a main export for Canada. The farmers reaped a small harvest that fall. Their seed had cost more than their harvest was worth.

The Great Depression had begun.

Black Blizzards

The next year was no better. Juanita, 12 years old at the time, remembered the annual Masonic picnic in July being interrupted by dark billowing clouds. Although the children were disappointed the picnic had to be cut short, their farming fathers were elated, anticipating the promising-looking rainstorm. But as the fierce hot winds blew up, the black clouds changed colour to dense sand. "Not one droplet of rain," Juanita reported sadly.

That year, the sometime fertile wheat belt was a dry, yellow wilderness. The dirt, continually worked by the farmers with ill-fated determination, crumbled to dust. One dust bowl farmer described sod he could barely hang on to: "The dry dust would just float away, like smoke," he said. "That dirt which blew off my hand, that wasn't dirt ... that was my land, and it was going south into Montana or north up towards Regina or east or west and it was never coming back. The land just blew away."

The relentless winds gathered the dust into immense storms that swept across the prairies in swirling "black blizzards." In January 1931, residents of Moose Jaw, Saskatchewan, experienced a dust storm so fierce that houses across the street from one another disappeared from view. The sky was either obscured or hazy with a yellow smokelike pallor. Lanterns had to be lighted all day.

The dust sandblasted everything in its path. It sifted into houses through cracks in windowpanes and under doors. Dishes had to be washed before they could be used. Cupboards had to be swept before dishes could be put away. Clothes needed a good shake before they could be worn. Juanita remembers her mother's prized Hudson's Bay blankets ruined and tearfully put away for good. Cleaning became an endless cycle of sweeping and shovelling dust.

Even breathing became a chore. Farmers wore handkerchiefs tied around their face when they went outside. Still, they couldn't avoid ingesting the insidious dust one way or another. It made its way into the few meagre meals, leaving food gritty and practically inedible.

As the wind sucked up moisture and light, the water shortage became acute. The ducks normally found in sloughs could fly away, but Juanita recalls wondering where the poor muskrats went.

Farmers persisted, but weather conditions conspired against them. Juanita recalled that if the dust storms didn't outright prevent seeding, they blew up later and undid all the work done.

Plague

In 1932 and 1933, the drought backed off and farmers got a reprieve. Juanita and her sister were thrilled to skate on the ice-covered sloughs in the winter months. But the precipitation was not enough to sustain the farms. Like the Depression, dust bowl conditions were spreading across western Canada and the Midwestern United States. In Canada alone, at least one-quarter of all farmland was situated within the dust bowl region.

Farming soon earned the reputation of being the slowest way to starve during the Depression. Even studious farmers like Howard could barely cope with the elements. "We were all in the same boat," he recalled, always watching the sky with hope. He couldn't believe it would get any worse.

Then came the first plague of insects. Watching clouds of grasshoppers blot out the sun, a fellow farmer reported, "They were in their millions, tens of millions and where they decided to stop all at once, then those farmers could just kiss that year's crop goodbye. If he had a crop ... and I'll tell you I've never seen a more terrifying sight."

Grasshoppers ate $30 million worth of crops in 1933

alone. They came down like hail, remembered a discouraged James Gray. "They grabbed everything and chewed it all up as soon as it stuck its head out of the ground. They even ate the clothes hung out on the line." In dust bowl folklore, it was said the grasshoppers would eat shovel handles and shirts off people's backs when they were finished eating the crops. Chickens and turkeys gorged themselves on grasshoppers, making their meat taste disgusting.

Four consecutive years of drought cleaned out most farmers' bank accounts and credit. Battered and broken-hearted, Howard added municipal councillor to his résumé, along with amateur vet and repairman, even though there was no money in the job. At least he was forgiven his taxes.

The official relief programs were far from adequate; there was no such thing as welfare yet. Eldest of Ken's 10 children, Albert was forced to abandon school and his family's own farm. He and several brothers hired themselves out as a threshing crew for 50¢ an acre. "We nearly starved," he recalled.

Help Needed

Out of sheer desperation, other families had to swallow their pride and beg for help. Howard was able to scrape together two dollars to lend a neighbour who needed a doctor for his son. But the neighbour had waited too long to ask, and his son died.

Jennie Hodgins of Perdue, Saskatchewan, wrote to

the prime minister to beg long underwear for her husband before he froze to death one winter. R. B. Bennett replied to many such letters, often sending a small donation from his own pocket. But his and Howard's good will was not enough to stem the drought or the Depression.

With no money to buy gasoline, many people removed the engine from their cars. They hitched a pair of oxen or horses to the front and called them Bennett buggies. "We had to make the best of what we did have," Juanita said, sighing.

The prolonged drought even spawned medical crises. Prairie doctors couldn't cope with all the blood poisoning working itself into every cut and sore because of lack of moisture. Juanita's mother permanently lost hearing in one ear when she couldn't get to a doctor to treat the infection caused by dust lodged in the ear.

In 1934, the dust and the wind only got worse, bringing with them other infestations — all of which destroyed anything green and growing. Like grasshoppers, gophers thrived. There were so many gophers eating their way through new growth and harvested crops, the government offered a bounty of a penny a tail. More than 1 million tails were handed over for the penny bounty during the 1930s. The gophers were of another use, too. Farm families boiled, baked, pickled, smoked, and fried the rodents.

Thousands of cattle had already starved, suffocated in the dust, or died from eating dirt. By autumn 1934, the federal government had to do something. Instead of importing massive amounts of feed for the winter, it began to ship starving livestock by train out of the area. Supervising the shipping of his region's animals, Howard was forced to put several "scarecrows" out of their misery. He knew they would not survive the trip.

In the worst-hit spots, the government took over former farmland, seeded it with perennial grasses, and turned it into community pastures for livestock. Much of the useless land had already been abandoned, but incredibly, some of it had to be taken forcibly from stubborn farmers.

Leaving It All Behind
The year of 1935 proved to be no better than 1934. The Lawrence family considered moving back to Ontario, despite their love of the prairies. Their village, Woodrow, was now a mere ghost of its former self. Juanita's friends had moved away with their parents, seeking literally greener pastures.

Farming colleagues like Jim and his wife Kate, who owned a piece of land halfway between Saskatoon and Regina, resigned themselves to their fate. Any optimism was gone. "We had no crop and we had no money," Kate said. "We didn't take off enough to give us seed for the next year."

The final blow for the couple was equine sleeping sickness. The disease, which causes animals to waste away, was carried by swarms of mosquitoes. When the vet told them their remaining horses were infected, Jim took each one behind a bluff and shot it, rather than let it suffer. With all their horses gone, Jim decided it was time to do what many of his neighbours had already done — sell the farm.

"He said there was no use going on," Kate remembered. "Everything was against us. We had no kids, so God was against us. We had no crops, so God was against us there too."

Jim and Kate sold their farm in November for $1500 to a Regina businessman. They sold most of their belongings at an auction for $200. "You had to make the break sometime," she said. "I'm glad we did when we did. That depression lasted four more years. Four more years."

Packing their few possessions into their Bennett buggy, they left their farm to the dust, along with whatever possessions they could not sell or take with them. In some unlocked abandoned houses, dishes and utensils sat on the table, covered in thick dust for years.

And Worse Still

The winter of 1935 blew in as the coldest winter recorded. Blizzards pounded the prairies. Saskatchewan recorded an average temperature of –32°C. Cattle froze to death. Juanita and her siblings were terrified they would face the same fate trying to make it home from their small school by sleigh. Regardless, the snow was a welcome sight. At least it was precipitation.

But the dust bowl had yet another surprise for beleaguered farmers. The summer of 1936 was the longest and hottest yet of the drought years across Canada. Hundreds of people died due to the heat that James Gray described "as if some-one had left all the furnace doors open and the blowers on." The average temperature registered over 38°C. Each day was hotter than the last. In Saskatchewan, only three days out of a six-week period dropped below 32°C. The record extreme temperatures of 1936 would stand for more than 30 years.

Dust bowl families started to head north to the more productive lands of Peace River country or, like Kate and Jim, west to the fertile Okanagan Valley. If they were going to starve, they could at least be warm. The 1936 census confirmed that 8000 farms in Saskatchewan and 5200 in Alberta had been abandoned. The dust bowl displaced about 300,000 people in total.

Between 1933 and 1937, the prairies received almost half their normal rain. By the end of 1937, farmers had lost their crops, livestock, livelihoods, and, in many cases, their homes. Water sources were bone dry. Grasshoppers, gophers, stem rust, and thistle had destroyed what little crop was left, and relief from the government was minimal.

When she was 19, Juanita had to move to the city to get work. Her father, a committed wheat farmer, reluctantly took on raising turkeys to help make ends meet. One family sold its 16-year-old daughter to a middle-aged man prepared to pay $500 for a wife. Times couldn't get much more desperate.

In mid-July 1938, however, relief seemed to be in sight. Black thunderclouds began to move across the prairies, followed shortly by rain. It fell for three days straight. But the relief was short-lived — and not nearly enough to revive the parched land.

That winter, snow fell and stayed. Southern Alberta experienced one of its worst blizzards ever. The 128 km/h winds filled the coulees with snow 15 metres deep. Drifting snow smothered thousands of yearling calves in the fields. Prairie people just couldn't win with the weather. Precipitation in this form was just as destructive as drought.

The spring rains returned in 1939, along with the dust bowl's final blow. Drought, stem rust, and grasshoppers destroyed half of Saskatchewan's harvest.

Hope Again

Then — suddenly — the drought was over. Juanita remembers the evening her father called the family out of the barn to see a double rainbow — its double significance not lost on anyone: "A rainbow was always a promise of something better to come."

As World War II began to revive the rest of Canada's economy, the rains filled prairie sloughs, ponds, and lakes. Plants appeared around their edges, followed by the return of songbirds and frogs. Amazingly, life returned to the dust bowl.

For the first time in 12 years, the burned-out, hailed-out, worn-out prairies yielded a bumper crop. Those who had toughed it out reaped the benefits of their patience and hardiness. Juanita's father and brother became prosperous on their large farm and installed electricity and a refrigerator at last. Albert Scheffelmaier and his family were able to buy a 200-hectare farm and finally earn a good living, too.

Over recent winters, as El Niño–inspired temperatures have risen, some of the prairies have again received less than half the normal snowfall and very little rain. However, now accustomed to the weather's unpredictability, and forced to implement alternative farming practices, farmers have been better prepared. In May 2001, Saskatchewan experienced record winds. If the same winds had blown across the prairies during the 1930s, even without drought, they would have stripped fields bare. This time they didn't. Farming techniques had changed in the prairies, but not farmers' tenacity.

Howard and Marjorie Lawrence continued to believe it was a wonderful country, and homesteading it had indeed been a good idea. "When people ask me about the Depression, I don't tell them about the hard times my mom and dad went through," someone else who lived through the dust bowl years admitted. "What I tell them is how the prairie can come back."

But, like the prairie land and its people, the weather — in its amazing extremes — is also irrepressible. Drought will no doubt return to the prairies, but will the dust bowl?

Chapter 4
Blizzard of the Century

A true blizzard is an unusual weather event that may occur as rarely as once a year in some parts of Canada. Its hallmarks are rapidly falling temperatures, high winds, and blowing snow causing low visibility.

The strong northerly winds make the blizzard the most dangerous of all winter storms — a winter hurricane, in effect. The low-pressure system that causes a blizzard does not necessarily bring fresh snow, but the fierce winds do their best to stir up what's there. They are responsible for a blizzard's signature whiteout conditions, lifting snow from the ground a short way into the air. If there's a lot of snow around, the effect can be magnified. But, for as intense as the conditions are, they usually don't last long.

Not only did the storm that hit the Niagara region in January 1977 last much longer than normal, it arrived quickly. Along with an unusual amount of loose snow around, the conditions combined to make the blizzard the most severe of the century. At least one man, Alex Mulko, didn't think he would live to talk about it.

Wall of Snow

The winter of 1976–77 had been a strange one. Not only had Lake Erie frozen, it had done so remarkably early. The ice that had formed on a calm and cold night in early December was so smooth that the dry, fluffy snow that had fallen nearly every day since did not stick to its 26,000 square kilometre surface. January had been cold, too, so the snow powder did not melt or stick together, but instead piled up loosely.

On the morning of Friday, January 28, heavy snow was falling again in Lowbanks, a community bordering Lake Erie. The wind had also started to pick up. At 8:00 a.m., Alex Mulko received a call from a friend who said his gas and water wells were freezing and he had no heat in his house.

Accustomed to wild winter storms, Niagara residents like Alex did not like to panic, but he did not take the weather lightly either. Once, he and his wife, Irene, had been stuck in a huge storm and were storm-stayed in Pennsylvania for three days. At the end of that storm, people were found dead in their vehicles.

Although in his 60s, Alex, a former wrestler, was in good

shape. He agreed to drive out to his friend's farm. As he hung up the phone, a strange feeling of dread came over him. "I said to my wife, 'I'm going for helping [*sic*] my friend but I'm afraid that I might never come back.'" Irene urged her husband not to go. Nonetheless, Alex dressed in three pairs of long underwear, winter hunting pants, three undershirts, hunting shirt, vest, hunting jacket, parka, and finally gloves and a hat.

The temperature had dropped to –18°C, but the wind chill pushed it to a frigid –51°C. Without much warning, the Arctic front was sweeping down from the north. The accompanying winds roared in, averaging 80 km/h, but with the strongest gusts recorded at 117 km/h. Even though snow was no longer falling, it was getting harder to see.

From his home on the shore of Lake Erie, Erno Rossi was observing a flock of Canada geese on the frozen lake. "Suddenly the geese all collapsed on their breasts onto the ice facing into the breeze. They then pulled their feet up into their breast feathers. Twisting their necks backwards, they then tucked their bills and heads into their back feathers."

Wondering why, Erno put down his binoculars and looked up. A white wall taller than his house was moving across the ice toward the geese and the first windbreak — his home. "That wall of snow hit my house with hurricane force and almost shattered the bay windows. The blizzard of the century had arrived."

Into the Storm

Meanwhile, at the farm, Alex and his friend had set to work clearing snow from around the well. They tried to thaw the well by burning straw, but the ferocious winds kept blowing the fire out.

As the wind and blowing snow got worse, Alex finally told his friend it was time to get inside. His friend refused. Alex gave up and left his friend to deal with the well. His premonition was bothering him and he wanted to get home.

By then, the westerly winds had lifted the massive amount of dry snow from Lake Erie and blown it toward the Niagara Peninsula. Trees and houses on the shore, like Erno's, acted as a snow fence, slowing the wind and depositing the snow. Whole communities on the lake's northeast shore were buried under snowdrifts 12 metres deep.

Alex drove from his friend's farm to the Number 3 Highway. Passing many cars already stuck in the snow, he turned onto Lakeshore Road, where the snowdrifts were the highest he had ever seen.

Within minutes Alex was stuck. He was only 3 kilometres from his house, but instead of walking home, he decided to wait out the storm. Alex couldn't find the candles or blankets usually stored in the car for such emergencies, but told himself it didn't matter. He was warmly dressed. If he needed to, he could run his car for a little extra heat until the blizzard calmed down.

Alex settled in to wait. It was 11:00 a.m. All he could see

beyond the hood of his car was a swirling white wall. The winds were growing stronger, and the visibility was dropping just as quickly. This was no simple snowstorm, it was a true blizzard.

By then, thousands of people like Alex were already stranded as highways and railways became impassable and airports were shut down. With so much snow accumulated on the lake, the local weather office was concerned about a catastrophe in the making and had set about warning the public. No one knew how long the conditions would last.

School's Out, and So Are the Snowmobiles

That morning, around 9:00, Doug Wilcox, superintendent of the South Board of Education, had taken an unusual call from the weather office. Normally, the school board wouldn't get a direct warning of a storm, but this was no normal day — the cold front bringing the storm was moving rapidly.

Doug and the other superintendents decided to send the children home. But as buses began to arrive at about 11:00 a.m., the blizzard's full fury smashed into the Niagara Peninsula.

Before long, buses were either stuck on the roads or trapped at the schools. About 2000 students were stranded at schools. Teachers and staff did what they could to keep students safe and comfortable. But when the power went out, the superintendents were left with no choice but to get their students evacuated.

When the storm started, the Niagara Regional Police had rented a handful of snowmobiles. They planned on handling the emergency calls themselves. But as the blizzard grew much worse than anticipated, the police needed help. They called the militia.

For the first time since World War II, the Lincoln and Welland Regiment was pressed into service. Nine regular Canadian army personnel joined the 156 reserve members to evacuate schoolchildren in personnel carriers and four-wheel-drive trucks to nearby houses or facilities that still had power.

Local snowmobilers, including Fred Butler and his son Randy, volunteered. Some helped the militia evacuate students. Others cruised roads, checking cars stranded by the growing snowdrifts. At first, most emergency calls were from people who needed to be evacuated or rescued. But as the hours passed, calls started to come from people without food and water. Throughout the storm, snowmobilers zipped between houses, schools, office buildings, hospitals, and police stations, ferrying food, water, and medicine.

Driving a snowmobile during a complete whiteout came with many risks. One snowmobiler smashed his sled into a house's chimney. The high snowdrifts also brought snowmobilers close to phone and power lines and a host of other hidden dangers. At one point, Fred stopped his snowmobile at the top of a drift and got off to scout what lay before him. Between blasts of snow, he saw a car parked in a driveway — at least 3 metres down. "I hadn't even realized that I was standing on top of a house," he said.

Friend in Need

Throughout the day, Irene Mulko waited for Alex to return. He had always called her when he was going to be late. Finally, at about 10:00 p.m., she convinced two neighbours who had been checking in on her to look for him. Her worst fear was that he was already dead.

Larry and an underdressed David set off on foot into the night, armed with Irene's wine. The radio had reported temperatures as low as –55°C with the wind chill. The snow was still swirling wildly, making it hard to see or even breathe.

Alex, like many others trapped by the blizzard, was sitting in his car waiting patiently for the storm to let up. He had managed to stay warm by running his car every half hour or so. However, as the snow buried the car, including its exhaust pipe, he was forced to stop. He knew that the carbon monoxide exhaust could kill him.

By 11:00 p.m., Alex began to feel the hard bite of the cold even with his many layers. He weighed his options again — either wait in the car for someone to rescue him or head out into the blizzard to find shelter. Since he couldn't even get out of his buried car, he was forced to wait. At least he was out of the wind and stood a better chance of being found. He knew Irene would worry and send help.

His fate sealed, Alex relaxed. The long day had made

him drowsy, so he decided to have a quick nap. What he didn't realize was that his drowsiness was a sign of hypothermia. Even though he was warmly dressed and in good physical shape, it was not enough to stop Alex from succumbing to the cold.

Four hours later, at 3:00 a.m., Larry and David found Alex's car. By sheer good fortune, one of them had stumbled over it, thinking it was a snowdrift. When they fell through the snow to the trunk and realized it was a car, the men pushed aside snow to peer inside with their flashlights. They were surprised to see Alex slumped in the driver's seat.

After clearing snow from around the door, Larry and David opened it to find Alex barely responsive. They washed his face with his wife's wine to wake him. By then, Alex had been in his car 16 hours.

Larry and David had found Alex, but they still had to get him to safety. How much longer could he last?

The Snowman

Larry and David got no clues from the now-strange landscape of where they were. Reluctant to wrestle their 250-pound friend out of the car when they had no idea where to take him, the two men left Alex in the car. They then ploughed through the deep drifts of still-blowing snow, looking for shelter.

Fortunately, only 15 metres from Alex's car, they happened upon the dark shape of the Argo home. Except for one bay window, most of the house was buried in snow.

Pounding on the window, the men woke up the Argos. With their help, they broke a window panel so they could scramble into the house. David, ill-prepared for sub-zero temperatures, refused to go back out into the blizzard. The storm had not let up, and he was certain Alex was already dead.

Larry, however, was not so convinced. Braving the storm, he trudged through the drifts until he found the car. Larry managed to haul Alex from the car, but he needed help dragging him through the drifts. Digging a hole in the snow, he rolled Alex into it to get him out of the roaring wind. Larry then disappeared into the whiteout while Alex, who had lost one of his gloves in the snow, lay on the verge of death.

Once in the house, Larry had to convince the still-frozen David to go into the blizzard again. Using the prairie farmers' technique for finding their way from home to barn in blizzards and dust storms, they attached a rope to the house and unspooled it as they went so that they could follow it back.

The two men managed to pull the hallucinating Alex through the extreme wind-chill conditions to the Argo home. When he was pushed headfirst through the window, the astonished Mrs. Argo said he looked like a weird kind of snowman. "His eyebrows were full of snow and his hair was frozen," she recalled. By the time the corpselike Alex was safely in bed, it was 4:00 a.m. He had been in the blizzard for almost 20 hours.

Alex spent the next day at the Argo house, drifting in and out of consciousness. His badly frostbitten hands and feet were swollen and painful. The Argos had called the police, who'd dispatched snowmobiles, but they'd failed to reach the house. The snowdrifts along the lakefront were simply too big for even snowmobilers to manoeuvre their machines around. After being buried alive, Alex was still trapped by the storm in a house without power, and he was succumbing to shock.

Recovery

As morning dawned on January 30, Major W. A. Smy, operations officer for the Lincoln and Welland Regiment, surveyed the lakeshore by helicopter. Not being able to reach the lakefront, the police had no idea how bad conditions were. They had only been able to go by descriptions they were given over the phone. The blizzard had created an absolute whiteout that had already lasted an incredible 24 hours.

From the air, Major Smy had a unique perspective of the storm's power. He could see that deep drifts had formed a thick belt along the lakefront. On either side of the snow belt, the winds had scoured the ground and the ice bare. "During that flight, I was astounded that the drifts out around Lowbanks were thirty and forty feet high," Smy said. All he could see of the Lowbanks church was the steeple.

Snow was still falling, but the whiteout had at least cleared temporarily. Once the helicopter was able to land on the bare ice close to the Argo place, Major Smy and the co-pilot had to dig from the eaves down to reach a window. With the aid of a stepladder, they got a heavily bundled Alex out of the house. Major Smy remembered Alex's hands looking like two little footballs and knew his feet were frostbitten, too. "I was amazed that he was able to walk to the helicopter."

Alex was in the hospital for five days before Irene was able to see him. Highway crews had started trying to clear roads, but she was still snowed in. She finally hitched a ride in a news helicopter that had landed to take pictures of their home.

Alex spent 18 days in hospital. His hands healed and his fingernails grew back. "Anyhow, I am safe. I am just so happy I have good friends who take risk of their life [*sic*] to help an old poor wrestler," he said. "I know that snow can kill."

Taking Off

The unusual blizzard conditions lasted for four days. When the sun came out, people emerged from their frozen snowy cocoons to find a surreal white landscape. The wildest, most stunning blizzard in Ontario history cost $300 million in repairs and snow removal.

Incredibly, no one died on the Canadian side of the border, thanks to the efforts of hardy Canadians like Larry and David and the Butler snowmobilers. Fred credits the storm for bringing out the latent courage in volunteers. "It's quite a thing to take on Mother Nature and come out the winner. I guess we learned a lot about ourselves in those conditions."

On the final day, Erno Rossi went to find the Canada geese he had spotted four days earlier. He took their photo shortly before they stood up from their hunkered-down positions, flexed their wings, and flew off. That's when he realized, "The blizzard of the millennium had ended."

Chapter 5
Wreckhouse Winds

The Atlantic provinces are home to some of the strongest winds in Canada. Newfoundland's Wreckhouse winds can reach hurricane strength and even merit separate weather warnings.

These southeasterly winds are a localized phenomenon that pound the Codroy Lowland, a broad coastal plain nestled between the Gulf of St. Lawrence and the Long Range Mountains, from autumn through early spring. Low-pressure weather systems circulating counterclockwise up the eastern seaboard funnel through the mountains' steep-sided valleys, creating a natural wind tunnel.

Compressed and squeezed, the wind bursts across the open plain with a sudden explosive force, bowling over anything in its path. Often, there's no warning that it's about to hit. Only the tangled, twisted tuckermore spruce and a few other stunted trees manage to survive in these frequent gusts that can reach 200 km/h.

Wind Power

Throughout the last century, Newfoundlanders have had limited success battling the wind's amazing power. Wreckhouse winds would indiscriminately tear roofs off buildings, and blow down fences, poles, towers, and aerials. They stripped storm windows from their mountings. Any door facing the mountains was locked when the wind was blowing, for fear of it being torn off. Locals knew enough to lie low or risk blowing away themselves. It was best to be in the most solid structure possible.

The U.S. Air Force realized the power of these winds during World War II. It had a radio base on the top of Table Mountain, the sentinel of the Long Range Mountains, that got hammered by a storm in 1944. Gale-force winds ripped the radar turntable and array from its base during the night. Ten men were forced to go out into the storm to try lashing the array back in place. A morning inspection showed that one of the concrete bases for the gantry sustained an incredible 30-centimetre crack. The air force had just discovered a powerful new enemy — Canadian wind.

Newfoundland's trains first encountered the true force of this enemy 50 years earlier.

The Newfoundland Railway

Before the rail line was built, Newfoundlanders lived predominantly along the coast and travelled almost exclusively by boat. While they were aware of the coastal winds, they probably were not familiar with the more remarkable winds inland. The construction of the Newfoundland Railway in the late 1800s introduced Newfoundlanders to these winds.

The Newfoundland Railway tracks curve north over the island, linking St. John's on the east coast to Port-aux-Basques on the west. When the railway was completed in 1897, it became the longest narrow-gauge railway in the world, 882 kilometres long. The tracks were spaced 100 centimetres apart, unlike the mainland, where tracks were usually spaced 142 centimetres apart. Railway builders chose the narrow gauge because it was cheaper and more adaptable to the rough terrain's steep grades and tight corners.

Stability, however, was not a strong point of the narrow-gauge railway. Rhoady J. Hickey, a railway engineer for 44 years, described the ride in a narrow-gauge locomotive as shaky. "They're pretty back and forth ... when there was no wind, you know," he said. "When you were firing, you had a job standing up in them going around the curves." He added that the narrow wheel base made it easier for the Wreckhouse winds to wreak havoc. "Trains blew off the track on many occasions during its 90-year operation," confirmed Mont Lingard, a railway enthusiast who chronicled the history of the Newfoundland Railway.

Passenger Train Number 1

In the railway's first years, trains ran sporadically during the winter. In 1898, the tracks were sometimes blocked by blowing snow in drifts 3 metres deep. The next year, the rail line was blocked for the entire winter. As a result, Wreckhouse winds remained an unknown entity until one winter morning in 1900, when Passenger Train Number 1 left Port-aux-Basques for the run to St. John's.

Passengers would have just settled in for the 28-hour ride when the train entered the Wreckhouse region. Tremendous wind gusts tore the train from the tracks. No one was injured, but the baggage and mail car was destroyed by a fire caused by the derailment. After this wreck, railway crews extinguished any fires burning in furnaces as a safety measure before entering Wreckhouse.

For four years, the railway tried to operate as normal, but the winds presented too much of a problem. In 1904, the Reid Company offered to build an alternate route into the Long Range Mountains, where the wind gusts were much weaker. The Newfoundland government nixed the idea because of its cost. Instead, the railway had to continue playing the odds. And the odds were not often in the railway's favour.

Airborne

On one occasion, a 20-car train was heading south for Port-aux-Basques. Near St. Andrews, the wind started to howl, and the crew argued about whether it was a southeaster. "The smoke was baffling everywhere, going this way and that way," recalled Alex Robertson, an engineer on the train. "We're going to get caught with our pants down," he warned his fellow engineer in the caboose.

Just north of Wreckhouse, a gust of wind Alex described as "a concrete wall" slammed into the train with a "WHOMP!" The crew managed to limp the train into St. Andrews to report the wind, then decided to continue their run. They hoped to leave the wind behind. But as one crewman from the caboose left the station house, he was picked up by the wind, carried about 6 metres, then slapped down onto the ground. Alex suggested the caboose crew ride up front in the engine with him, but they declined — a decision they would soon come to regret.

As the train crossed a bridge over MacDougall's Brook, unbeknownst to Alex in the front, five rail cars and the caboose were suddenly torn from the tracks and thrown into the air. The caboose landed on its side on the frozen brook at the edge of the Gulf of St. Lawrence.

Worried, but unable to see anything amiss in the dark, Alex decided to ride out the growing storm south of the bridge in a place known as "the hole." A low ridge to the east of the tracks offered some shelter while he waited for the wind to die down. However, the men in the caboose barely survived the long, cold night, water lapping against the roof. If the caboose had taken a second roll, it would have ended up in the gulf — and the men would likely have drowned.

As Alex experienced, engineers were rarely at risk of becoming airborne when a train entered Wreckhouse, unlike the crew and passengers. The sheer mass of locomotives would keep them firmly rooted to the rails. "The wind used to blow the cars all over but the engines were pretty good, they'd hold on," Rhoady said. "But the cars would be gone, you know."

Engineers like Rhoady would often unhook the locomotive from the cars and steam into Wreckhouse to test the winds. Sometimes engineers would ask permission to leave the cars on the siding, take the locomotive home, and come back for the rail cars when the winds died.

Losing Battle

The locomotives were not invincible, however. Their weight may have kept them on the tracks, but the wind still found ways to create problems for engineers. Gusting wind could slip down the smoke stack in the coal-burning locomotives and push it out through the cabin grates. "We were hand-fired," Rhoady explained. "When you opened the fire-box door ... the flames used to come back in the cab ... You'd had to be careful, you know. That's why you couldn't run in that wind. There's no way you could fire an engine."

Even after the railway converted its coal-burning locomotives to oil, engineers still faced difficulties. The winds could snuff out an oil fire and leave the train stranded. The train would not move until the engineers got the fire burning again and built up a head of steam. If they didn't do this carefully or in time, wind gusts could easily lift up the box cars and throw the rest of the train, even flat cars, off the tracks.

For at least 30 years, the railway fought a losing battle against the wind. When the annual losses hit more than $1 million, abetted by the post–World War I slump, the government of Newfoundland took over the railway's operation. Then it was up to its officials to find a solution.

Along Came Lockie

In the early 1930s, a resident of Wreckhouse — Lockland "Lockie" MacDougall — came to the rescue. The MacDougall family had settled in the Wreckhouse area around what was known as MacDougall's Gulch in the mid-1800s. The railway had been built only a quick minute's walk from Lockie's house around the time he was born, in 1896. Under the Long Range Mountains and a short distance from the Gulf of St. Lawrence, Lockie — like his father before him — farmed, raised livestock, and trapped.

But Lockie had a special talent. Living in the heart of strange wind country, the local legend had learned to read the wind's habits. It was said he could smell the wind. Lockie's daughter Kay described how: "He watched the clouds and the waves on the sea and the way the winds blew ... He watched animals all his life. Animals can always tell you when it's going to be a storm." Lockie knew that when he saw clouds moving from east to west, Wreckhouse winds were likely on their way. The sound of the wind could also tell him when it shifted and trouble was brewing.

Lockie soon found himself with a new job. The railway offered him $20 a month to warn the stations when he thought the winds were too strong for trains to safely make it through Wreckhouse. The company installed a crank-arm phone in his house.

When the winds started blowing, even when they woke him in the middle of the night, Lockie would call Port-aux-Basques and St. Andrews and tell the conductors to hold the trains. "Whenever the wind came, he was in charge," a veteran train engineer recalled. The trains were not to move until Lockie gave the all-clear. They would chain the train down to the rails and stay put.

No Perfect System

The system worked well, but it was not perfect. The railway continued to lose trains to the winds, mostly due to human error. A conductor who decided to ignore Lockie's wind warning experienced the folly of his decision when the 22-car train was ripped from the tracks. Some conductors refused to stop at Wreckhouse, fearful of tempting fate, whether Lockie gave the all-clear or not.

Sometimes, not even Lockie could predict when it would be safe for trains to run, the winds gusted so sporadically — and trains would be derailed. When rail cars did come off the tracks, Lockie would often walk the tracks to check on the crew. At times, he had to bring frightened and nearly frozen people back to his house to wait for the winds to die down.

Exactly how many trains Lockie delayed, or how many rail cars he saved, is unknown. One knowledgeable source suggested Lockie likely delayed hundreds of trains over his years of service.

Gale-Sniffer Extraordinaire

Lockie became famous as the "human wind gauge." Appreciative staff of the Newfoundland Railway gave him the fancier title of "gale-sniffer extraordinaire." Lockie, however, had a third title, one that he preferred to use. As Rhoady, who knew the man, said, "He'd never give you his name. He'd always say, 'I'm the wind man.'"

After forecasting the winds for the Newfoundland Railway for 35 years, the wind man passed away in his Wreckhouse home in 1965. Eventually, he was replaced by an anemometer — an automated wind gauge. Sitting on a utility pole visible from the site of the MacDougall house, which had burned down in the early 1990s, the gauge fed wind readings directly to the yard master's office in Port-aux-Basques. This new, sometimes unreliable, technology didn't change the weather though. Trains still had to wait out the wind, sometimes for up to 56 hours.

By the time of Lockie's death, construction of the Trans-Canada Highway had virtually killed the railway anyway.

Wreckhouse Winds

Built roughly parallel to the rail line in 1965, the new highway brought bus service and transport trucks to the island. Still, motorists, like the train riders before them, take their chances when the winds blow. Although large bright orange signs warn drivers at either end of the Wreckhouse section, winds usually upend 12 to 15 transport trucks in the ditch every winter.

Technology may have replaced the human wind gauge, but it still can't contain the ferocious and unpredictable Wreckhouse winds. Newfoundlanders just know to watch, wait, and batten down the hatches.

Chapter 6
Red River's Lakes

ccurring at virtually any time of year, floods have affected hundreds of thousands of Canadians in many regions, rural or urban. Floods can be Canada's costliest natural disasters in terms of property damage. They are also a recurring catastrophe, much to the chagrin of Manitobans. Because of its peculiar geography and climate, Manitoba has suffered the most — and the most often.

The province's Red River and Lake Winnipeg are descendants of a continental ice sheet that melted almost 10,000 years ago. The enormous glacial lake that resulted left the Red River Valley even flatter than the rest of the famously flat prairies.

The 877-kilometre Red River is prone to floods in the

spring because its southern headwaters in Minnesota thaw before the Canadian north is usually free from ice. When the Red River tries to flow north into Lake Winnipeg after winter, it can get blocked by the ice downstream. Then, not being able to rise up banks, as with a normal river, any extra water of the Red spreads outward immediately. To make matters worse, the non-porous clay layer below the valley's rich topsoil isn't good for absorbing overflow.

Unlike other extreme weather disasters in Canada, the flooding of the Red River is a slow-moving catastrophe. The river's average slope is only 10 centimetres to the kilometre and the fastest it goes is about 6 km/h. Its power is in its size not its speed.

The First Floods
The Crees tried to warn early settlers of the Red River's destructive potential. The Earl of Selkirk's 400 Scots came anyway to settle the Hudson Bay post named Fort Garry. The flood they experienced in 1826 had the honour of being the first documented flood and the one against which all subsequent ones are measured.

With rain falling at a rate of 30 centimetres every 24 hours, the river rose slightly more than 11 metres above the riverbed and created a choppy 90-kilometre-long lake that covered the plains. There was no advance warning or dike protection, so chaos soon reigned.

Settler Alexander Ross recalled the scene in his journal:

"The people had to fly from their homes for their dear life, some of them saving only the clothes they had on their backs ... The shrieks of children, the lowing of cattle, and the howling of dogs added terror to the scene ... Hardly a house or building of any kind was left standing in the colony."

Governor George Simpson doubted anyone would stay to rebuild, and about half the disheartened did leave the area. But the rest of the tougher prairie settlers surprised Simpson by staying, and he rebuilt Fort Garry downstream at a widening in the river. Until the railway was built, the Red River was considered the best highway in the area, triple-decker paddlewheelers cruising it regularly.

As the settlement grew, subsequent floods caused more damage. Alexander Ross, one of the self-described "wretched inhabitants" stubborn enough to remain on the flood plain, helped rebuild with drainage ditches. They did not stop the pattern. In 1897, two men made the news by shaking hands in downtown Emerson, a town on the Red close to the American border. One was on a steamboat, and the other on the second floor of a hotel. The Red River had become a lake once more.

Finally, the question changed from "Should the settlement move away from the floods?" to "How can floods be moved away from the settlement?" This question would be posed again and again over the next century.

The 1950 Flood

By 1950, many floods later, Winnipeg had nonetheless grown from Fort Garry into Canada's fourth largest city, with a population of 400,000. With 700 square kilometres of its richest farmland, "Red River Gumbo," the Red had become a willing servant to 1 million Canadians and Americans living along its banks. They had become accustomed to regular spring flooding, but had been spared a major disaster for a couple of generations. The province was thus not prepared for what came that spring.

By April, weather conditions — a long, severe winter with deep snow and ice and a late, cold, snowy spring — had aligned to produce extreme flooding conditions. Earthen and wooden dikes went up to protect farms. Portable grain augers, looking strangely like short giraffes, were adapted to pump water instead of grain and send it back over the dikes. During the dust bowl years of drought, farmers had created ponds to collect the meagre rainwater. Now, ironically, animals struggled up the artificial hills of these prairie dugouts to escape certain drowning. Along the river's most southern parts, veteran farmers began to ship out livestock and prepare their families for flight.

Schools put students to work building sandbag dikes before sending them off with bags of homework in the event of evacuation. The art of filling sandbags and stacking them into dikes again became the most important skills for survival on the Manitoba flood plain. While the temporary sandbag dikes slowed the leaks, and water gushed out of every basement pump, one by one, the earthen dikes along the river collapsed.

Black Friday

The worst day, dubbed Black Friday, was May 5. The day began with the official warning that "previous estimates of the flood level are likely to be exceeded." The flood was already the worst in 90 years, 8.2 metres above normal, with the river still rising.

The flood had also claimed its first victim. Lawson Alfred Ogg, a 24-year-old accountant, was one of the hundred thousand volunteers who had spent the last nine days sandbagging Greater Winnipeg. That Friday, the temperature had gone down to freezing, and a strong wind kept thrusting the flood waters against the flimsy temporary dikes. As Lawson's barricaded back door collapsed, he was sucked into the basement, where he drowned. Three hundred luckier families escaped the wall of water that desperate night with only the clothes on their backs.

Premier Douglas Campbell finally proclaimed a state of emergency after the disastrous day. This helped to organize the relief effort, which was now anticipating the mass evacuation everybody dreaded. Disaster relief for victims had traditionally been the responsibility of private agencies such as the Red Cross, but it too was overwhelmed and not sufficiently organized for such a large-scale emergency. Never before had so many Manitobans needed its assistance. The siren atop the Winnipeg Free Press building, mute since air raid exercises during the war, wailed its warning.

Operation Red Ramp

In the largest military operation ever in peacetime, 5000 personnel, some of them temporarily called back into their World War II uniforms, assisted the local volunteer flood-fighters. The army's recent war experience gave it the expertise and discipline badly needed in a province just starting to realize what it was up against.

For Operation Red Ramp, food was stockpiled, and emergency passes and ration cards printed. The army built more dikes and manned pumps. Soldiers rescued 20,000 stranded people from 13,000 flooding farms and the roofs of homes along the Red with whalers and amphibious personnel carriers nicknamed ducks.

Amid the chaos, some people were confused as to what to save — one evacuee brought a curling trophy instead of her jewellery. Arn McEwen was supposed to be meeting his wife at the movies one night, but had discovered his street was being flooded, so he went back to save something. "There I was, almost being swept away by the force of a tidal wave, guiding each step carefully, a fish-bowl in one hand and a bunch of bananas in the other and the river up to my waist. I remember thinking: if I step off this sidewalk I'm a goner." Like many people, Arn had never imagined the flood would reach his house. Now that it had, it showed no sign of stopping.

Evacuation

More than 500 square kilometres were already under water, and the crisis was threatening to continue for up to four more weeks. Then it began to snow. This precipitation was the final straw — it prompted the largest evacuation in Canadian history to date: 80,000 city residents (adding to 20,000 already out of their homes).

The province had never experienced a disaster of that size — and there was no model to follow. The closest thing for the worst-case scenario was Operation Blackboy, adapted from London's (unused) evacuation plan prepared during the Blitz of World War II.

Near the city, evacuations started with St. Vital — which, until then, had been considered a non-flood area — then moved on to Winnipeg on May 11. In St. Boniface, the 425 residents of a seniors' residence were loaded into army ambulances that had to be towed through more than a metre of water by diesel tractors. At the station, they were put on trains to hospitals in Regina.

By May 12, the river had reached over 9 metres. Everyone watched and waited. Two days later, on Mother's Day, it was still rising. Operation Blackboy and a large-scale city evacuation seemed inevitable. On May 17, spring convocation at the University of Manitoba was held even though no graduates attended. The residences had been taken over by refugees from the south.

The Last "Flood of the Century"?

On May 25, the sun came out. The river had reached its crest, 9.2 metres above normal. It appeared as if the rest of the city's residents would be able to stay in their homes. About 10,000 homes, one-eighth of Winnipeg, had been flooded. Almost one-quarter of the city had been evacuated, in addition to those from towns farther south.

By the end of May, Operation Rainbow was arranging for the 100,000 evacuated victims to begin returning to their houses in the Red River Valley. Facing a clean-up job while exhausted from almost two months of floodfighting wasn't going to be easy — but they were prairie people.

Arn McEwen, who had saved his goldfish, demonstrated typical Manitoban mettle. Desperate to see how his house had fared, he managed to borrow a canoe to paddle to it. When he tried to open his front door, he couldn't. Then he remembered he had locked it. "Why not? Good for keeping the fish out," he could still joke.

In terms of the amount of ground covered and river height reached, the 1950 flood was the fourth biggest in Manitoba's history, but the damage it caused was amazing — insurance claims alone reached $50 million (more than $600 million today). The most expensive flood to date had made Manitobans realize they needed more than earthen dikes and sandbags to protect the growing city from regular flooding. Although they knew this wouldn't be the last flood, they wanted to ensure it was the last "Flood of the Century."

Floodway

A popular refrain of the 1950s went "If I'd-a known you was coming, I'd a built a dike." Dikes were still so much on the minds of the people of Manitoba that during the provincial election of 1959, Duff Roblin successfully campaigned for the job of premier on a promise to Metro Winnipeggers that "their property and means of livelihood will not again be disturbed by the rampage of flood water."

A couple of years later, the province dug a 47-kilometre-long and more than 100-metre-wide floodway to divert the Red River's overflow east around the city and into Lake Winnipeg. Building "Duff's ditch" required excavating more dirt than was excavated for the Panama Canal.

Constructing this marvel of modern engineering was not easy either. Earth-moving machines easily became stuck in the Red River's sticky liquid mud. Engineers had to cope with seven railroad bridges, five major highway bridges, oil and gas pipelines, and six hydro rights of way — all crossing the Floodway. Even though it was supposed to save $3 for every dollar spent, some critics regarded it as a waste of expropriated land and money.

The Floodway was completed in 1968, in time to save Winnipeg from flooding at least 18 times since, fulfilling

Duff's promise. Without it, 80 percent of Winnipeg might have been under water. Even during the 1974 spring flood, when the Red and Assiniboine Rivers crested almost simultaneously, the Floodway performed well.

In the meantime, other methods were examined to protect flood plain dwellers south of Winnipeg. During the 1970s, permanent ring dykes were built around eight towns in southern Manitoba. Like upside-down moats, they protected those communities from seasonal flooding. Many were built as high as the eavestroughs of town buildings. Permanent dikes were also built around 700 rural homesteads.

Even sandbagging went high tech. In 1994, Winnipeg bought a Sandbagger, a machine that could fill 90 sandbags per minute. The city thought it was ready for anything the river could throw at it. But the biggest test was still to come.

The 1997 Flood

Once again, in the spring of 1997, the valley was threatening to flood. "The enemy was the Red River. And the enemy did not sleep. It was relentless," claimed Major Doug Martin — a third-generation Canadian Armed Forces floodfighter.

Despite the lessons learned and the preparations made, history seemed destined to repeat itself. Few could remember the 1950 flood, their grandparents' flood. One Winnipegger had blithely knocked down a dike that interfered with her view of the river, putting her whole neighbourhood at risk.

All the signs were there — an extremely bad spring flood

in 1996, twice as much snow that winter, and unusually large amounts of snow in February. According to the more sophisticated forecasting in place, the 1997 flood was threatening to exceed the 1950 flood by two or three times. The province stockpiled a million sandbags, set off explosives to get the river flowing, raised and reinforced dikes, and thought that everything would be okay — if it didn't snow.

Snow

In early April, 50 centimetres of heavy, fresh snow blanketed the already record-breaking snow pack of 250 centimetres, followed by a deep freeze. Hydro lines snapped, and flood crews were diverted to snow removal. Another year of heavy rain and snow could not be absorbed by the rock-hard frost layer. "It's been a long winter. We didn't need this," said Larry Whitney, the provincial flood coordinator. "Thank God we've got the Floodway." But would the Floodway do the job against what was already being billed as the new Flood of the Century?

Manitobans watched events upstream with growing concern. On April 17, the annual breakup of the Red River in Fargo, North Dakota, resulted in massive flooding, surpassing 100-year-old high-water records. The city next in line along the banks of the Red — and only 200 kilometres from Winnipeg — was Grand Forks.

Already half under water, Grand Forks was evacuated April 19. When fire, caused by the flood short-circuiting power systems, which in turn ignited broken gas lines, ravaged its downtown core, firefighters couldn't reach it. After witnessing the $1 billion carnage in North Dakota on TV, Manitobans closest to the border, and next on the line to greet the enemy, were on the edge of panic.

Manitoba premier Gary Filmon, a former hydraulic engineer, knew too much not to be worried. His flood team tried some new tactics, including the "Swiss cheese experiment" — drilling 40,000 holes into the river ice to break it up. The last tactic was opening the Floodway, with the hope it would once again do its job. On April 21, the former premier and folk hero Duff Roblin sounded the loud siren that warned Winnipeggers that the Floodway was to be opened. The Floodway was helped by secondary dikes, plus 6.5 million sandbags nicknamed Red River perogies.

Lucy and Bernie Gray weren't taking any chances. Their 40-acre thoroughbred farm in Grande Pointe had never been in flood danger, and computer simulations of how much water to expect and what it would do indicated they had nothing to worry about. Nonetheless, they, their seven children, their children's spouses, and their friends all helped sandbag the family home. The dike they built was even higher than the flood's projected peak.

As the family watched the flood waters come closer, they kept sandbagging. Soon they had to get the sandbags in by boat, as their house became an island. Despite Lucy's teary, desperate pleas, the supply depot never had enough bags for her. When their neighbour's house went under, they added his then-useless sandbags to their dike and kept their fingers crossed.

OOTW

Volunteers also came from the 8000 soldiers of the military operation nicknamed Noah — comprising the largest military endeavour since Korea. One soldier commented that the OOTW (Operation Other Than War) was "safer than Bosnia and the food's better."

Safer maybe, but floodfighting was undoubtedly still dangerous. One soldier, who had returned unscathed from Croatia, lost his badly burned hand when his boat touched an underwater electrical cable. A 14-year-old boy lost his life after being sucked into the sewer system. Two other people died as a result of the flooding.

Floodway and dikes notwithstanding, there was still "potential for the entire valley to be evacuated," announced Premier Filmon ominously on April 22. A state of emergency was called for all towns along the river's shores. The river was swallowing everything in its path, and thousands were placed on 24-hour evacuation alert. They grabbed medications, passports, and other identification and turned off their gas and power before locking their doors and reporting to the Red Cross for instructions. With sustained high winds in the forecast, the situation likely wasn't going to get better.

Brunkild Dike

With the city's growth and the water's volume, a new worry unique to 1997 surfaced. Experts predicted that the widening Red River could flood Winnipeg via its now exposed southwest flank. Crews had only 72 hours to build a mammoth new dike with clay, mud, straw bales, limestone, giant sandbags, and derelict cars and school buses. The Brunkild dike, named for the small town 50 kilometres southwest of Winnipeg, was finished barely in time — the river continued to move slowly but stubbornly toward the city.

Built to protect Winnipeggers, the Brunkild dike may have sacrificed other Manitobans. Just 25 kilometres south of Winnipeg, Ste. Agathe sat on elevated land and didn't flood even in 1950, so didn't merit a ring dike. In 1997, its entire population of 500 had to be evacuated. Some ignored the evacuation order to madly sandbag the community. But after midnight on April 29, a wall of flood water covered the town. The workers had only 15 minutes to flee.

In St. Norbert, which also lies just beyond Winnipeg, Joseph Riel was busy fighting the river as his forebears had, although none of them had ever experienced anything of this magnitude. Joseph helped sandbag the church from where his great-grandfather, Louis Riel, had launched the 1869 rebellion that led to the founding of Manitoba. Then he had to flee himself.

After sandbagging non-stop for three weeks, Lucy Gray and her family were finally forced to evacuate at the

A truck sits in flood water in downtown Ste. Agathe. April 30, 1997.

last minute. The next day, their farm was submerged, just 2.5 kilometres south of the Floodway. As its suburbs were swept away by "the red sea," Winnipeg knew it was in trouble.

On to Winnipeg

The Red was so high already that boats could not pass under the bridges in downtown Winnipeg. Bitter winds, now changing direction, made whitecaps smash high against the fragile dikes. An enormous inland sea of 2000 square kilometres was strangling the city on two sides. Temporary dikes were leaking. Convoys of trucks and armoured personnel carriers patrolled city neighbourhoods, and amphibious craft thundered throughout the city, still trying to shore up dikes and assist evacuees.

Six thousand of the city's 650,000 residents had already had to leave. One resident joked darkly on her answering machine: "Hello, I'm not here right now because the entire city of Winnipeg has been swept away by the flood. Leave a message and I'll get back to you when our ark grinds ashore on the crest of Mount Ararat."

Then, just like in 1950, in the midst of the worst of it, it snowed.

The New Flood of the Century

This time, the additional precipitation did not make matters worse. By May 1, the danger was contained when the river finally crested. The evacuation order was cancelled. At the flood's height, the Red had become the largest river in North America, covering more than 5000 square kilometres, an area the size of Prince Edward Island.

The city's defences had held, even if at the expense of some of the rest of Manitoba. The 1997 flood had indeed claimed the Flood of the Century moniker from its 1950 predecessor. The crest would have been at almost 10.5 metres, 5 metres above channel capacity. It was more than a metre higher than in 1950 and sufficient to cover every centimetre of Winnipeg.

Since the Red River Valley had been better prepared with its dikes, and Winnipeg with the Floodway, the worst did not happen. In the end, the flood caused at least three deaths. Property damage was estimated at as much as $500 million, in addition to $400 million for fighting the flood. But the Floodway prevented potentially $6 billion in damages and total evacuation of Winnipeg. An expansion of the Floodway is now in the works.

On the 50th anniversary of the 1950 flood, the University of Manitoba's graduating class of 1950 finally held its missed commencement. But despite their resiliency and increasing success at outwitting the enemy, Manitobans living along the Red River continue to watch it each spring, resigned to the fact that they will always have high water.

Chapter 7
Hurricanes — in Canada?

Hurricanes are large rotating storms that brew in warm tropical oceans, where the hot, moist air fuels their fierce winds and rains. Although not as fast as tornadoes, hurricanes are much larger, with radii of hundreds of kilometres, and can wreak more destruction. Rated on a scale of 1 to 5 — depending on wind speed (beginning at 120 km/h), storm surge, and damage — they can be weak to devastating.

Canada's decidedly non-tropical climate *should* make hurricanes unlikely. Yet, surprisingly, the country experiences tropical storms an average of four times a year, with the Atlantic coast being the most battered. One that struck off Newfoundland in 1775 killed thousands of British sailors.

Usually, hurricanes have lost much of their strength by the time they hit land. The resulting rain and winds are more typical of a moderate thunderstorm, just one that lasts longer.

Hurricane Hazel

The eighth hurricane of the late summer–early fall season in 1954 spawned near the island of Grenada in the tropical Caribbean. After category 4 Hurricane Hazel demolished Haiti, it headed for the U.S., where it killed 100 people and caused such extensive damage that martial law was declared.

Then the leftover wind and weather headed north. Meteorologists expected it to hit Toronto around October 15. By the time Hazel reached the Canadian side of Lake Ontario, it was unlikely to be classified as a hurricane. Certainly, nobody *expected* a hurricane in Toronto. The country's most heavily populated region is nowhere near a path known for tropical storms. At 200 metres above sea level, Toronto is 500 kilometres from the nearest ocean where hurricanes lurk.

However, disasters often occur when a combination of factors, including the element of surprise, exacerbate a dangerous situation. Hazel was originally labelled "a weakening storm." Local weather reports predicted only rain and winds. But this storm was rejuvenated when it connected with a low-pressure system.

During the afternoon of October 15, paperboy Bob Stuart was delivering the 5¢ newspaper containing the misleading weather predictions. Stopping at his house to change his soaking wet clothes three times, he took longer than usual to finish his route.

The torrential rain slowed the evening rush hour too, as deep puddles collected in underpasses. The Toronto Transit Commission's subway, which had just opened that year, turned out to be a far better way to travel than its aboveground streetcars. But puddles were starting to collect in the underground stations, too. The rain blew forward, backward, and sideways. Sometimes it even seemed to blow upward. Winds gusted to 120 km/h, then died down, only to pick up again.

Late that Friday evening, even as the storm re-intensified, people were not aware they were experiencing a hurricane. Listening to the radio was no longer the habit it used to be after World War II, and television was still new and rare in many households. Even if Percy Saltzman — the first Canadian TV meteorologist — had mentioned the possibility of more severe weather on his brand-new show, few would have heard his warning. One person who did hear some unbelievable news reports trickling in on the radio said he thought he was listening to "one of those Orson Welles plays." A hurricane in Toronto? Impossible.

The reports were not fiction. The torrential rains that

accompanied Hazel had flooded the city's waterways. The year had already been the rainiest in Canadian history, but few people in Toronto realized what that much rain at once could do. In less than 24 hours, Hazel dropped 300 million tonnes of rain on top of previously saturated ground.

Toronto's flat landscape, interspersed with ravines and valleys trickling toward Lake Ontario, exacerbated the situation. With all that extra water, normally mild-mannered rivers like the Humber and the Don became fast-moving freight trains, overflowing their banks and spilling out into residential areas.

At that time, no civil emergency organization existed in Toronto to cope with the unexpected catastrophe. If the precipitation had been snow, there would have been equipment, experience, and personnel in place.

For the flooding of Hurricane Hazel, the city was forced to rely on its police and fire staff. These were the days when police officers patrolled on bicycles and used pay phones to check in with headquarters. Firefighters were mainly volunteers, paid 75¢ whenever they were called out from their regular jobs to put out a house fire. They didn't expect to be dealing with floods.

Washed Away

Cliff Sherman and his six-months' pregnant wife, Marion, lived a few hundred metres from the Humber River with their two-year-old toddler, two teenagers, and 70-year-old grandfather. The night of October 15, Marion heard a strange noise. Looking out their bedroom window, she saw a 2.5-metre wall of water coming straight at their farm house.

The ice-cold water surrounded and engulfed the house in minutes. Even out the back door, the water was chest high, so escape seemed impossible. Standing on a piano, Cliff punched a hole in the ceiling. Then he helped all six members of the household — elderly to infant — squeeze into the tiny crawl space.

Through a hole cut in the gable, they all watched helplessly as a familiar barn floated by. Still attached to it was a tethered horse, neighing frantically. Soon, their house left its moorings, too, and started to float on the river. All around them, they could hear neighbours screaming for help from inside or on top of their houses.

The Shermans were eventually rescued around 3:00 a.m. but taken in separate boats to opposite sides of the river. It was three days before Cliff found Marion and the children. He was lucky — many of his neighbours went permanently missing in the river.

Some people didn't believe the seriousness of the situation. Joan Price's grandmother, "a strong-willed old lady," refused to be rushed out of her house even though the water was up to her knees. She insisted on being fully dressed, corset and all, before she would accept help to leave. By the time she was pushed and pulled to the top of the hill, her house had been washed away.

Lives Lost

Rescue did not come in time for many unfortunate people. Bridges over the Humber River collapsed later in the night, and a tidal wave 6 metres high roared down the valley. As the water overflowed the collapsing river banks, houses near the banks were swept down the now massive river.

Raymore Drive — built on a flood plain next to the river — disappeared. Used to flooding in spring but never in fall, many of its residents were either asleep or did not heed warnings to flee. Some clung to their rooftops, screaming to be saved. Firefighters working up to their chins in the bitterly cold water tried to get life ropes to those stranded on rapidly disintegrating houses.

Fireman Bryan Mitchell described it as something out of a horror movie: "The incredible roar of the water, like the roar of Niagara Falls. It was a gigantic flood, with smashed houses and uprooted trees bobbing like corks, everything going down the river so fast. Houses crashing into the sides of other houses, people everywhere screaming. And then you couldn't even hear the screams anymore." He added sadly, "For everyone we got out, there was another we couldn't."

At least 36 people were missing and presumed dead after the worst single incident of the Hazel disaster. The river also claimed the lives of five volunteer firefighters that night.

Seasick ... Aboard a House

Hurricane Hazel affected a huge area, more than just the

city of Toronto. North of Toronto, the large market garden community of Holland Marsh turned into one vast lake with millions of floating onions. Only the church steeple was visible. Most of the community's 3000 residents had to flee to higher ground and shelters once the water submerged their properties.

One family had just immigrated to Canada the year before, escaping terrible floods in Holland that had killed thousands. The de Peuters couldn't imagine a flood in Ontario — as far as it was from the ocean — so they didn't worry at first when they noticed water seeping up their steps. They barricaded the door as the water rose higher.

Soon, the de Peuters found themselves with no option to flee. Their house left its foundation and turned into Noah's ark for an entire frightening night, spinning and tipping. The family had to run from one side of the house to the other to keep it level. One of the 12 children became violently seasick.

The house finally "landed" 5 kilometres from its original location, held in place only by a field of carrots. Rescue came from surprised passers-by. One unnamed hero managed to swim out with a rope and tie it to the house. Another man with a canoe pulled himself along the rope in the choppy waters to liberate the large family. It took him seven careful trips.

Receding and Rebuilding
The next day, as the water receded, volunteers searched for survivors and bodies. Boy Scouts and the army that had

helped Winnipeg after its famous 1950 flood were called in to help. One poor Scout, supposed to be spending the day selling apples for the Scouts' annual Apple Day, was instead helping comb the river banks. He discovered his own father buried in the mud. Other bodies were found in trees or drowned in cars. Some were never found. At least 81 people died in the storm. One baby was orphaned when her parents and brother drowned that night.

Even with the army's help, the city needed more than two months to recover and rebuild after the worst weather disaster in its history. Holland Marsh was eventually drained and resettled. Flood plains became parks. Emergency plans were updated and modernized.

As happens whenever a hurricane causes such devastation and loss of life, the name Hazel was not to be used again for future hurricanes. Torontonians hoped they would never have to deal with a hurricane of *any* name again.

Hurricane Juan

Like Toronto, Halifax had reason to be complacent when it came to hurricanes. Tropical storms come calling an average of three times a year, but they are usually not of hurricane strength by the time they reach Nova Scotia. The coast's topography, its numerous bays, and high tides all limit the potential danger from tropical storms. The cooler temperatures of northern Atlantic waters help to dissipate potential storm energy, and the Gulf Stream often steers storms away.

Hurricanes — In Canada?

Before September 2003, the province had not been hit directly by a hurricane in 40 years, experiencing only some leftover weather. A few degrees to the left or right, most serious storms spare Halifax. Usually.

On Thursday, September 25, the tropical depression named Juan officially qualified as a hurricane when its wind speed topped 120 km/h. By Friday, the storm was moving slowly north from Bermuda, accompanied by strong winds and heavy rain. A storm surge (when a hurricane sucks up water, raising the ocean's level) was expected along Nova Scotia's east shore. The forecasters also warned that regional southeasterly winds could be strong following the storm.

On Saturday, Chris Fogarty, a weather forecaster working at the Canadian Hurricane Centre in Nova Scotia, noticed a more ominous sign — an unusual increase in the temperature of Halifax's harbour water. He knew tropical storms — which draw energy from warm waters — usually begin to weaken when they reach cooler water. This storm looked as if it was *accelerating*.

By then, forecasters at the Centre were warning of the risk of coastal flooding — if the water surge reached 1.5 metres. Warnings of wind and as much rain as 80 millimetres were also broadcast. Juan, or its aftermath, could reach landfall by Sunday evening. There was potential for tree damage, floods, and power outage — all normal occurrences accompanying high winds, which Nova Scotia had experienced many times before.

A youngster rides his bike in front of the wood from shattered wharves in Prospect Village, Nova Scotia. The small fishing community lost all its wharves during Hurricane Juan's passage. October 1, 2003.

On Sunday, checking satellite imagery, forecasters could tell that the storm bearing down on Halifax was still a hurricane. Whatever land a hurricane hits first gets the worst of its power. Halifax, and the area around it, was about to be hammered. The airport was closed and all flights cancelled. Coastal flooding was inevitable — waterfront buildings and homes had to be evacuated. Other residents were advised to batten down their hatches.

Battening Down the Hatches ... or Not

"If you want to live near the ocean, you've got to be prepared to pay the price every now and again when it acts up," declared Murray Houghton, who had experienced the leftover winds and water of Hurricane Hortense, which blasted Cape Breton Island in 1996. But he didn't expect the price to be so high as he cleared off the floor of his garage and stocked up against a certain power outage.

Stephen Hatt also knew to put away his deck furniture at his home on the coast in Mahone Bay and move the cars to a higher location. He boarded his east- and south-facing windows. Stephen, a professional meteorologist, had lived through the aftermath of a weakened Hurricane Blanche 28 years earlier. He had some idea of what to expect.

At one commercial marina, Alderney, where high winds were always taken seriously for their destructive power, boat owners were trying something new. Not only did they pull some boats out of the water and use a spider web of ropes to tie boats to docks and docks to shore, they extended dock pilings with floating risers. This way, the docks could rise and fall with the tide and, with any luck, escape sinking or major damage.

Apart from meteorologists and boat owners, most Haligonians didn't worry. The common sentiment was that the weather was rarely as bad as forecast. Windsurfers joyfully took advantage of the wild winds on Sunday afternoon.

More interested in experiencing their first real hurricane than keeping themselves or their property safe, thrillseekers also braved the winds on the waterfront. Some even tried to sneak past patrol officers for an ideal vantage point in the exposed Point Pleasant Park, overlooking the entrance to the city's harbour. But park officials remembered all too well the damage caused by Hurricane Hortense and other wind storms. They had closed and evacuated the park by 6:00 p.m.

Juan Hits Land

By late evening, a state of emergency had been declared so federal, provincial, and municipal emergency measures organizations could roar into preventative mode. Anticipating evacuations and damage control, Halifax was on standby.

The wind that preceded the hurricane whipped up the ocean. Waves reached almost 20 metres. The storm surge set a new record — almost 3 metres — causing extensive flooding of the Halifax waterfront. Hundreds had to abandon their waterfront homes. The park's boardwalks and grassy areas were replaced for 10 metres by beach and stone from the surge.

The wind picked up at 9:30 Sunday evening. It ripped power lines from poles and blew out hundreds of transformers. Despite the power company being on storm mode three days before, three-quarters of the province — 300,000 people — were blacked out. By 11:00 p.m., the power was out in many parts of the city and region.

At 12:10 a.m., Juan made landfall between Shad and Prospect Bays, 20 kilometres southwest of Halifax. The worst of the storm hit between then and 3:00 a.m. Juan was rated category 2, its wind reaching 151 km/h, gusting to 176 km/h. The diameter of the eye was 35 kilometres. The worst of the wind, the eastern eyewall, went right over Halifax's harbour.

First to feel the hurricane, most harbour marinas and boat owners were neither as well prepared nor as fortunate as the Alderney Marina. Boats at yacht clubs were tossed around like beach balls, ending up on land or out at sea. Several large sailboats sank in the harbour, only the tops of their masts visible after the storm. At Alderney, no boats sank, and three-quarters of their boats escaped damage.

At Stephen Hatt's place — on the coast but farther from the storm's centre — water flooded the whole property. "The waves were breaking up against the deck and water was spraying up from the deck boards like fountains."

Halifax resident Derek Weir had deliberately parked his new car under the one huge old oak that he was certain would withstand any force. He was in bed when he heard the tree fall, crushing his vehicle.

John Rossiter, a paramedic on duty near a hospital that busy night, wasn't so lucky. He had just called his father in Newfoundland and received a warning to be careful.

John had laughed, pointing out that his dad had been okay throughout his own dangerous career as a firefighter. Then one of the top-heavy, 20-metre trees in Camp Hill Cemetery fell over without warning, crushing both the ambulance and John. He was the first of two people killed in their vehicles during the hurricane.

The wind ripped off half the roof and windows of the largest city hospital, forcing the removal of 200 patients. A section of a four-storey apartment building partially caved in, and hundreds of terrified tenants had to flee in their nightclothes. Two university students were the subjects of a dramatic rescue. When their apartment roof caved in, water and debris blocked their regular exits, and police officers had to smash their way through other apartments. One of the girls had to be treated for shock in hospital.

A newspaper reporter remembers never being more terrified in her life as she tried to make her way home. Walking to her van was the first challenge. "It was pitch-dark, but there was an eerie glow in the sky, broken glass all over the sidewalk ..." Then she had to negotiate her way through trees and wires lying everywhere on the road. Blocked, but desperate to get home, she decided to try to get through the last few blocks on foot. "It must have been raining quite hard, but the primary thing I remember was the wind. It was deafening ... inescapable, constantly coming at you ... I was almost hyperventilating."

At the Canadian Hurricane Centre, located on the 19th

floor of a waterfront building, meteorologists monitoring the storm had secured tape over the almost floor-to-ceiling windows. But it was the ceiling that started to come apart. Already working on emergency power, the staff decided to retreat to a lower floor. But once in the stairwell, they noticed that the building was swaying, so decided to descend to the safety of the lobby instead.

Amazingly, some Haligonians claimed to have slept through the whole thing — although it would have been hard to ignore the sound of houses shaking and rattling in the wind. Most people, including Tamzen Black and her family in the south end of Halifax, terrorized by the relentless noise, were forced to retreat downstairs and away from windows. Tamzen did not know exactly what was happening outside until the next morning, when she saw her neighbourhood looking "like a war zone, unbelievable, trees totally uprooted."

Taking Stock
The next day, the usual grey misty dawn brought a ray of sunshine, then a torrential downpour, as if to show that Juan was not yet finished with Halifax. All non-essential workers were told by the city to stay home. Schools, universities, and most stores closed since they were without power. The city turned strangely quiet. By noon, the sun came out again and the city was able to take stock of the damage.

Before the hurricane, Point Pleasant had been Halifax's jewel and Canada's largest urban forest. A diverse forest of both native and Old World transplants, some of its trees were remnants of the Acadian hardwood forests that had been in Nova Scotia since the ice age. Of its 80,000 trees, 90 percent were impacted and an estimated 75 percent destroyed. It was the worst damage to the urban canopy since the Halifax Explosion of World War I. One report said it looked as if a giant had used the park as a bowling alley. Another treasured public park, the venerable Public Gardens, was also almost totally flattened.

Outside the city, farmers and fishermen were badly hit, too. Jim Lorraine's greenhouse was intact, but not where he had left it. The wind had carried it 100 metres, taking out telephone poles and trees along the way. His barn had lost its roof and his corn crop was beaten to ruin. Docks, wharves, and fishing shacks near the coast had been shredded like matchsticks. James Gray lost 550 lobster traps, sucked into the sea. He faced rebuilding his livelihood before the short season opened in seven weeks.

Other families fared even worse. Two fishermen were lost at sea during the storm. While one family's power was out, they used a candle that started a fire, killing the mother and two of her young children. Juan had now taken, directly or indirectly, seven lives in total.

More than 85 millimetres of rain fell that Sunday night in the city. The resulting flooding caused traffic problems and general chaos due to downed power lines, broken glass, and roof debris. Near the famous Commons park, the water was knee deep. The storm even toppled trains from their tracks, taking out 1.3 kilometres of track.

Order to Chaos

Although getting around was difficult, hurricane sightseers came out in full force, along with people trying to restore order to chaos. With typical Maritime spirit, the community of Victoria Park put on a barbecue to feed the power-less. Neighbourhood residents emptied freezers and solicited donations even before the Salvation Army could take over. Campfires inspired singalongs to restore spirits. The military was called in for Operation Splinter, making the volunteers' work easier. The good weather that commonly follows a storm also helped the clean-up effort.

The city rebuilt and recovered, but some things will never be restored. When Point Pleasant reopened a year later, regular visitor Judy Fraser said that seeing what was left of the park's acres of woods made Haligonians want to cry.

Hurricane Juan had packed the biggest punch this century in Nova Scotia. The estimated cost to the province is more than $100 million. Because of Juan's deadly impact, Canada officially requested that the name Juan, like Hazel, be retired. However, Nova Scotians were not allowed to forget the name for long. In February 2004, another major storm brought the province to its knees — it was nicknamed appropriately White Juan.

Chapter 8
Hail Alley

hailstorm may be an intriguing weather oddity, but it is among the most regular and costliest of Canada's extreme weather events. Pea-sized hailstones can wipe out an entire year's crop and a farmer's livelihood, while golf ball–sized hail is capable of doing spectacular damage to urban areas in just a few minutes. Hailstones as large as baseballs have even been known to cause injury and death.

One section of the prairies, called Hail Alley, has the highest frequency of hailstorms in the *world*. The triangular region sits southeast of the Rockies between Edmonton and Calgary, stretching east into Saskatchewan. Canada's largest hailstone on record — 290 grams and the size of a grapefruit — landed in Cedoux, Saskatchewan, in 1973. Calgary, at Hail

Alley's southern and most active end, has experienced nine massive and destructive hailstorms in the past century.

While damages can be greater from other natural disasters, hail is one of few extreme weather phenomena that might be manipulated. Property owners and insurers, especially in Hail Alley, have long been motivated to try. Says one resident who has experienced nature's fury up close, "I like all kinds of weather. Anything but hail. I hate hail."

Calgary 1991

On September 7, 1991, Jim McIvor was driving through Calgary's northwest around 7:00 p.m. when he noticed the sky was black. He didn't expect anything more than a good summer thunderstorm, but all of a sudden, the road and the city beyond his car's hood disappeared. A dense wall of hail, mixed with rain and sleet, obliterated his view and assaulted his car. It sounded like the car was being pounded with ball bearings. "The noise was amazing," he said. "It was like being in the car with the radio turned on as loud as it could go. It was just unbelievable."

Jim pulled into a parking lot and stopped under a tree, hoping it would shelter his car. Instead, the hailstones knocked branches onto his windshield.

The storm quickly filled the parking lot with 30 centimetres of hail and slush. The landscape transformed into a bizarre out-of-season white. Jim's car was covered with dents. Its soft chrome trim looked as if someone had beaten it repeatedly with a round-headed hammer.

Graupel (snow pellets, or soft hail) and ice pellets fell on all parts of the city, but north of the Bow River was particularly hard hit with hailstones. Anyone caught outside rushed for cover. The hail was not only deafening and frightening, it ripped at exposed skin.

From one side of the city to the other, chunks of ice the size of softballs pounded gardens into the ground, stripped trees bare, and shredded shingle roofs. Calgarians cowered in basements away from windows and the noise rattling the roofs and their nerves. Normally, hail fall lasts only 6 to 10 minutes, but this continued for an incredible 30 minutes. For residents of Calgary, the giant pummelling machine seemed to go on forever.

The hail broke windows, punched holes in aluminum siding, and pierced lawn furniture. Golden Acre Garden Sentre, in Calgary's northeast, was practically destroyed when golf ball–sized hailstones crashed through the glass roofs covering its nearly 4 acres of greenhouses. Fortunately, no one was injured in the mess.

The stones plugged storm drains, and the rain mixed with hail quickly swelled into flash floods. The rushing water popped 15 storm-sewer covers off as it gushed up onto roads, filling the low spots, including major intersections and underpasses. Trapped drivers scrambled on top of their cars to escape the rising water. What was normally a quick drive out of the city took some drivers two and a half hours on slick streets blocked by debris, stalled cars, and small, newly formed lakes.

Rain swept hailstones downhill to accumulate in deep drifts. Some Calgarians braved the piercing cold pellets to shovel clear their drains and low-lying areas, fearful of consequences if they didn't. Others waited the storm out and hoped the hail would stop or melt quickly, but the melting hail then flooded garages and basements with metres of water.

Afterward, more than 60,000 claims for damages were filed with insurance companies. The $450 million in property damage did not even include damage to crops on farms around Calgary. The 1991 storm lasted only half an hour, but it was the most destructive hailstorm and one of the costliest weather events in Canadian history.

Thunderstorm-born

The topography of southwestern Alberta provides the ideal climatic basis for the intense thunderstorms that can create hail. Because the sun is so intense at upper elevations, cumulus clouds often develop in the clear blue summer mornings and grow vertically along the east slopes of the Rocky Mountains throughout the day. As clouds reach a colder altitude, the vapour condenses into supercooled water droplets — in other words, tiny hailstones.

Alberta's combination of cool air and hot sun creates particularly strong updrafts that bounce the newly formed hailstones around in the storm's centre, giving them time to grow. Each time a hailstone rises, another layer of ice is added. It falls when it becomes too heavy for the updrafts. A hailstone can become so dense that it can hit concrete at 100 km/h and not shatter.

Calgary 1996

Five years later, two more destructive hailstorms hit Calgary — on July 16 and July 24. Once again, Calgarians faced hail's heavy impact and suffered.

The first storm was by far the worst weather event Janice Fercho has ever endured. An avid gardener, Janice saw the late afternoon storm rolling in from her home on the city's western slope and moved as many plants and pots as she could.

Then she waited in absolute silence and perfect stillness under the eerie black sky. "As I watched, the heavens opened up with a terrifying ferocity, every leaf, petal, and all signs of life were mercilessly stripped from each flower, shrub, and tree in my yard. After every plant was laid bare, they were then pummelled to the ground with what was easily two feet of hail."

In the city, the hail and water instantly clogged storm sewers and flooded streets. Drivers had to take turns trying to make it through axle-deep puddles without stalling. Others slid into the ditch, where they were forced to wait for the hail and slush to melt.

Even the services that can usually be relied on in

emergencies were affected by the wild summer weather. Calgary's light rail transit was brought to a stop when a construction site's earthen walls caved in near the tracks. One of the hospitals flooded. The hail and high winds knocked out 911 service in the northeast.

Anything left unprotected outside had little chance of surviving the double attack unscathed. If the hail hadn't decimated Calgarians' roofs during the first storm, it finished the job on July 24. Like every second home-owner in his neighbourhood, Paul Kostyan needed a new roof. But there was nothing he could do about his trees. Huge branches littered his backyard, and what branches were left intact had been stripped bare of leaves. "It looked as if someone had pulled all the leaves, put them in a blender, and dumped the mixture on the ground," lamented Paul.

At one car dealership, the hailstorms did at least $1 million of damage to cars on the lot. Fifty cars were written off. So many cars needed extensive repairs that auto-body shops were kept busy for months. The one-two punch of the storms had ravaged the city with damage estimated at almost $400 million.

Farmers' Peril
Farming in Hail Alley has always been hazardous. Farmers plant their crops in the spring, hoping they can harvest before the agricultural "white plague" comes along. "It's one of the biggest gambles as far as a farmer is concerned," said

Don Alexander, a farmer who watched his livelihood get beaten to the ground.

In 1996, Don lost 100 percent of his crop. "You just don't get your wages that year," Don said. "And you have all of your expenses. You pay your fertilizer, your gas ... and you don't get a cent out of it." All that remained of Don's crop after the storm passed was a neatly shorn field of stubble.

Because hail damage is frequently sporadic and insurance expensive, the gamble increases. Some farmers play the odds and weigh the balance between having crop insurance and not having it. Often, crop insurance payouts barely cover expenses.

Weather Modification

Experimentation with weather modification began in Europe in the 1800s. In Alberta, the first attempt to control weather was in 1956, with the provincial government's hail suppression research project. In an attempt to diminish the size, and therefore the impact, of hailstones, airplanes seeded clouds with smoke particles. The results of the 30-year research study were inconclusive, so hail suppression was discontinued in 1986.

However, premiums for crop insurance rose afterward — sometimes as much as threefold. For the three-year period before the project ended, the losses reported by home-owners totalled $18 million. Over the next three years, that amount jumped to $113 million. The fifth year after the cloud seeding stopped was 1991, the year of the disastrous hailstorm. Still, the idea of weather modification needed more ammunition.

After the third major hailstorm that decade, insurance companies as well as victimized farmers and home-owners in Alberta had the ammunition they needed. The hail was carrying increasingly more physical and economic clout.

In 1996, after the massive amount of damage to personal property was tallied, Alberta's insurance industry established the Alberta Severe Weather Management Society. The following year, the society contracted Weather Modification Canada (WMC) to seed thunderstorms by plane, much like the original 1956 program.

WMC employs three high-performance planes for cloud seeding. The planes are armed with ejectable flares and wing-mounted "burn in place" flares that, when ignited, release billions of silver iodide smoke particles. (Silver iodide has a crystalline molecular structure similar to ice.) The smoke particles compete as nuclei for the water droplets forming in the clouds — increasing the number of hailstones and theoretically decreasing their size.

Not every storm is seeded — only the ones that are at the right stage. And of these, only storms that are threatening Calgary or Red Deer are seeded — the project's sole mandate is to reduce damage in urban areas. It is the world's first and only hail suppression project designed to protect urban areas.

Hail Busting

WMC pilot Mac MacQuarrie has been seeding thunderstorms around Calgary since 1996. A former air force pilot with 46 years of flying experience, Mac is one of about 12 pilots in the world specializing in hail suppression. It can be dangerous work, but the risks are always calculated. "Each thunderstorm is different. We consider them living things, and each visual interpretation and approach is different."

Normally pilots like to avoid all thunderstorms. Turbulent air can tear a plane's wings off. A lightning strike, the static electric charges in clouds, and the potential for icing at high elevations all threaten a pilot's good judgment, as well as his life. But the only way to effectively seed a thundercloud is to fly under its base or above it, in updraft areas where hailstones form. This can be a jarring ride.

"Well, it saves me a trip to the fair," joked the society's project director and pilot Jim Renick. "It's got a little lift to it and a few bumps ... you don't take a cup of coffee in with you." That "little lift" can reach more than 1200 metres per minute. "It can make you lose control, it can damage an aileron and then it can be all over," added Jeff Pomeroy, another veteran WMC hail-buster.

Jeff said he was "messed with" once when he flew into a storm embedded in a larger thunderhead. Losing all visuals, he then got too close. He recalled, "The first hail strike was like taking a big kettle and hitting it with a spoon next to your head." Then he was pelted from every direction with 5-centimetre hail.

Knowing hail can come right through the windshield, Jeff told the co-pilot to get down and cover his head. He himself ducked behind the console. "I banked hard away from the cell and put the nose down into a 2500-foot-per-minute descent." Fortunately, Jeff's fast plane took him out of the hail within six seconds, but it came out heavily pockmarked. Fighting the weather is dangerous work.

Is It Working?
Whether cloud seeding is effective has not yet been proven scientifically. Some farmers worry seeding will inhibit rains. Some scientists suggest that it could backfire — provoking bigger and more numerous hailstorms or generating more powerful storms.

Despite these concerns and criticisms, while there have been hailstorms, not one has been as destructive and costly as the 1991 storm. In fact, Alberta's insurance industry has seen hail damage claims halved since the project started. "The people who are paying the bill are happy," Jim reported.

They're so happy that, in 2000, Alberta's insurance industry extended the original five-year pilot project. "They're paying a couple of million dollars a year for a project that could be saving them $50 or $70 million a year. It's like buying a lotto ticket in some sense," Jim said. "You can't afford to and you can't afford not to." Insurance, like weather and hail busting, is full of risks.

Chapter 9
Firestorm

Fire is a natural part of the wilderness, but as Canadians live in greater numbers and closer proximity to forests, fire becomes dangerous and unpredictable. The summer of 2003 witnessed the most destructive fires in Canada's history, the second-largest evacuation of people — and the costliest natural disaster ever for British Columbia.

BC at Risk

British Columbia's history has been entwined with fires and forests, especially in the central and southern interior, where summers are hot and dry and the growth plentiful. Nature used to take care of any oversupply: regular fires thinned out tinder and dead trees, allowing the forest to flourish.

But as towns and cities have grown and encroached on the wilderness, and as people have moved to more rural areas, they haven't wanted fires, even controlled fires, to threaten their homes or change their views. So for the last 50 years, 10,000 hectares of forest floors in BC, covered with combustible undergrowth, have been untouched by fire, ripe for catastrophe.

Recognizing the high potential for interface fires — fires in areas where forests adjoin homes — BC's auditor general in recent years has recommended fire prevention. The government, however, continued to put aside funds for fire-fighting only.

Fire Season Comes Early

In 2003, after the province's warmest, driest spring in 74 years, the fire season started earlier than usual with fires burning near Kamloops and Vernon in the Okanagan. The region had had three dry summers in a row, with barely a trace of moisture. In Kelowna, it had rained on June 22, then almost two months had passed without any more rain.

Near the city's southeastern outskirts, 79-year-old Ronny Dixon didn't need to hear the radio reports to know that air quality was poor. The smoke from the distant fires made her hoarse and short of breath outdoors, so she resigned herself to staying indoors.

Ronny's daughter Anne Corey, visiting from New Zealand, was concerned enough to suggest escaping the area for a while, but Ronny was sure the weather couldn't last. Having survived a war and, more recently, heart surgery, she wasn't the type to complain about smog. As soon as a little rain fell, she could look forward to golfing again.

Instead of rain, fire came to Kelowna.

Two-Headed Monster

Shortly after midnight, on Saturday, August 16, lightning struck a tree in Okanagan Mountain Provincial Park, a huge wilderness park south of the city on Lake Okanagan. The columns of smoke were spotted from Peachland, directly across the lake.

The tree then exploded and, with help from ferocious westerly winds, sent gusts toward Kelowna. The local fire information officer, Karen Cairns, called the fire "a double-headed monster." Because of its location on the point, the flaming tree sparked fires going both east onto the rest of the park and west toward Kelowna. One of the fires was easily put out, but the other, although tiny, was harder to reach. The park's terrain also caused erratic wind behaviour, which didn't help the situation.

The buildup of dry tinder on the forest floor, combined with gusty winds, helped the fire travel quickly. By 3:00 a.m., the fire covered 10 hectares. Before dawn, the fire was at Rank 5, the second-highest rank of danger.

Helicopters came in to drop the first load of fire suppressant to help firefighters on the ground. For two and a half hours, air tankers dumped 39 loads to beat the fire back to Rank 2. Then they were redeployed to the 800 other fires burning in BC. They thought they'd caught this one in time. But by 1:00 p.m. on Sunday, the fire roared back to life, and the remaining ground crew pleaded for more resources. The risk to the largest city in the Okanagan was now acute. The water bombers returned, but it was too late. By evening, the hills of the park were ablaze, providing an orange and yellow spectacle for tourists and residents watching from across the lake. Unaware of the fire's seriousness, boaters got in the way of bombers skimming along the lake's surface to refill their tanks.

The Monster Grows

Strictly as a precaution, six families in the homes closest to the park fire were evacuated. As they left their driveways, they watched the red glow approach, estimating it to be 6 kilometres away. Their neighbours were placed on evacuation alert and had to be ready to leave the area if the fire worsened.

That ally of fire — wind — picked up unexpectedly and turned it back toward Kelowna, burning 1200 to 1800 hectares in two hours. As the fire came within 300 metres of the nearest homes, more people near the park had to be evacuated Monday.

On Tuesday, August 19, the temperature rose to a blistering 40°C, with gusty 80 km/h winds in the forecast. On the ground, 100 firefighters were busy soaking houses in the threatened residential areas. Overnight, the fire doubled — burning 95 percent of the park and destroying all of its precious and rare plants, including trees of three different ecosystems, and endangering its plentiful wildlife. The fire had reached Rank 6, the most dangerous rank of fire.

But the real concern was whether the fire would remain in the park.

Firefighters worried there was nothing more they could do — they'd never seen a scenario like this before. A fire of the most severe ranking had never threatened a Canadian city before. As one firefighter said, "Nothing stops a Rank 6."

The firefighters still tried. Bulldozers cleared wide paths for fireguards designed to stop the fire from spreading by starving it of fuel. Containment lines were built around the perimeters of properties closest to the wilderness. But burning embers jumped Chute Lake, just outside the park, and flames came within 50 metres of a Kelowna home. They were beaten back on the ground and by air. Nine helicopters buzzed overhead, buckets dangling.

It Won't Happen to Us
While most people in south Kelowna, including Ronny, were placed on alert, many residents continued to believe the fire couldn't threaten their city. Falling chunks of hard ash the size of golf balls weren't enough to stop golfers, who watched from the golf courses as planes and helicopters dashed over the flaming, smoking hillside.

Ronny's visiting daughter, Anne, was a little more concerned. "I don't think anyone was fully aware of the potential looming danger. There was a bit of an 'it won't happen to us' mentality," she recalled. For her, the scene was eerie, reminiscent of another strange time in her adopted country. "It was like watching the volcano Ruapehu spew, not knowing if the worst was yet to come. In New Zealand, I never saw flames, just the smoke ... but there too, I thought it was weird to see people still doing normal stuff like biking and running!"

With ash filling the sky and burning their eyes, Anne was relieved when her mother's golf course community started to take action. Organizing golf cart patrols, residents took turns keeping watch for sparks landing in their area. That Wednesday night, there was a vivid purple sunset, then the sky got really black. "That's when I knew it was getting closer," Anne recalled.

The next day, Ronny finally succumbed to Anne's wishes. With a small overnight bag, they went to the airport. Fortunately, Ronny was able to get on one of the few flights out. No one else in her community was allowed back home after that day. The roads were blockaded for the residents' safety — evacuation had begun.

Evacuation

On Thursday evening, the fire reached Kelowna. Sounding like a 747 taking off, flames broke through the 50-metre-wide fireguard a mere 3 kilometres from a thousand houses.

Sirens wailed through the nearby neighbourhoods. The police knocked on every door. "Time to leave, right NOW," officers instructed on megaphones.

Ten thousand people were evacuated that night. Packing their cars with photographs, scrapbooks, family heirlooms, anything irreplaceable, they joined a mass exodus. A panicked traffic jam resulted. In their rearview mirrors, evacuees could see the fire bearing down on them. Strangely though, nobody honked.

However, even with the looming danger, some disobeyed the evacuation order. As his wife and daughters fled, one man said he couldn't leave the home he had built himself. His fleeing family thought he was crazy.

That night, 15 houses were destroyed. Devastated Kelowna firefighters felt they'd hardly had a chance. Three firefighters lost their own homes. One of them, Johnny Kelly, had been on his way back from vacation when he heard about the fire. He reported for work immediately, then heard his house was gone. "I was trying to focus, but I had a real hard time," he admitted. He didn't blame his colleagues: "If those guys couldn't stop it, then nobody could have."

Fellow firefighters were pouring in from Alberta and around BC to help out, saying, "Whatever it takes to help, we'll do it." Locals donated food, water, and clothing and offered shelter to volunteers and victims.

The fire's fierceness, and of course the property loss, had also grabbed the attention of politicians, bringing them on tours. But what Kelowna needed was more help, not more tourists. The worst was yet to come.

Black Friday

On the morning of August 22, later dubbed Kelowna's own Black Friday, the fire had grown to four times the size of Vancouver's Stanley Park, about 400 hectares. Additional help arrived in the form of still more firefighters — 600 from the BC Forest Service, 350 from the military — to relieve the exhausted locals, along with bulldozers, helicopters, water tankers, and giant Oshkosh fire trucks.

The wind had increased to 70 km/h. A wall of flame 8 kilometres long was now bearing down on Kelowna. The assistant fire chief described it as "a monster that spat out balls of fire."

By the middle of Friday afternoon, a huge black cloud hung over the city. Instead of hoped-for rain, a cold front was threatening to add even stronger winds to the crisis. Pieces of bark ripped off trees. Pine cones turned into exploding missiles. Those small tornadoes and the 2000°C heat disintegrated the evacuated houses instantly. Lightning added to the surreal scene.

In the thick of the battle, firefighters were forced to make terrible decisions they'd never considered before. Working frantically to control whatever they could, they had to let one side of a street burn to save the other. While working a hot area, crews often couldn't see one another or even which way to run, if retreat was necessary. Sometimes they just had to give up. The strangest sight was emergency vehicles rushing *away* from the fire, sirens wailing.

In one hot spot, Kelowna firefighter Shawn O'Reilly, a veteran with almost 30 years' experience, recognized the futility of his team's efforts and prepared to withdraw. It was already dark at 5:30 in the afternoon when he gathered his crew around a truck. All of a sudden, "there was a real rumble and it just flashed all around us and everything went orange, and then everything was on fire. There was nowhere to go." Flames 70 metres high trapped them.

Surrounded by the firestorm's heat and exploding trees, the desperate crew dropped to the ground, faces in the grass, gasping for air. As the fire rolled over them, some vomited, while others were on the verge of blacking out.

Their only hope was to make a dash for safety in their truck. They drove through a wall of flames. "Some guys didn't think they were going to make it," remembered Vancouver firefighter Ed Pickett later. One of his colleagues was on a cell phone yelling to his wife, "We're going to die!"

Miraculously, no one lost their life on that Black Friday, although the toll was high in heat exhaustion, burned throats, and critical-incident stress. Few came away completely unscathed, physically or mentally, that day. After his night from hell, Shawn said, "I never want to see that again."

The 238 houses the firefighters lost that night were reduced to smoking craters. Only debris and the acrid burning smell of plastic were left — melted garden gnomes, children's toys, and a dishwasher filled with dirty dishes still waiting to be washed.

Fire Chief Gerry Zimmerman called it the roughest time in Kelowna firefighting history. Overwhelmed with his responsibility for so many lives, he didn't even know at the time that his son had been one of the trapped firefighters who'd almost died.

Bracing for More

After Black Friday, the firefighters' morale dropped to an all-time low. They thought they'd just lost the biggest battle of their lives. The city of Kelowna thought differently. Citizens erected a tall cardboard sign that read "Thank You, Firefighters" on Dilworth Mountain in the city's centre. An offhand comment by Zimmerman about his men being thirsty prompted children to tote beer and cookies in their wagon to the fire hall.

Despite the support, a sense of dread prevailed. Four hundred firefighters braced for stiff winds and a repeat of the previous day. One-third of Kelowna's population had evacuated — to motor homes in parking lots, friends' homes across the lake, hotels. It was the second-largest evacuation in Canadian history, and the largest in the shortest time.

At the evacuation centres, residents registered their whereabouts so worried friends and relatives could know they were safe, even if their homes were not. Phones were often jammed with overuse or were out of order.

Staying in touch and up-to-date on the fire's horrific progress became part of the evacuation experience. The whole city stopped for the daily 11:00 a.m. broadcast.

Returning Home ... If You Had One

The all-important weather gave everyone a breather for a few days to count their losses. On Sunday, August 24, Chief Zimmerman personally met evacuees from the burned areas to give them the news. He displayed keyed maps — if a house was shaded white, it had been saved, if it was black, it was gone — as far as they could tell. The worst-hit areas were difficult to map. All house numbers had been destroyed, so the driveways had to be counted instead.

Warren Saari was lucky. "I've got a home! I thought [my house] was gone. I felt like I was going to puke. Then I was searching the map and there it was!" he yelled, pumping his hands in the air.

A devastated Dennis Hostland lost everything. He had been driving to Vancouver when the order to evacuate came. "Everything was in there, with the exception of some photos," he moaned.

On Monday, buses were organized to take home-owners back into their destroyed neighbourhoods. Residents strained their necks to look at the surreal scene from bus windows. Some properties were ash pits — brick and stone chimneys remaining as two-storey monuments to what had been. One side of the street was charred but the other side untouched. The winds died down enough to permit 6000 to return home at the beginning of the week. Almost 16,000 were still evacuees and 20,000 more on alert. Orchardists went back in to try to save $1 million worth of fruit ready for harvesting.

Over the next few days, more were allowed home. The prime minister and premier flew over the area, then met with evacuees and firefighters. Money for relief poured in. The Salvation Army and Red Cross had collected so much from Canadians that they had to ask them to stop.

The Monster Reawakens

The prevailing sentiment seemed to be that life must go on. As the evacuation centres emptied, schools were preparing to open, desperate to restore some normalcy to life in the Okanagan.

By the end of Labour Day weekend, all but 70 evacuees were home. Workers had removed fallen trees, charred electrical wires, and damaged telephone poles, and most of the electricity and gas had been restored. Looking forward to getting home, Ronny Dixon flew back from Calgary, after almost two unplanned weeks away.

But after a more subdued Labour Day weekend than usual, the fire dragon reawakened. With still no rain or cool weather to slow the beast, gusty winds shifted the fire back to within 5 kilometres of the city.

A second round of evacuation for 3200 residents in

south Kelowna included Ronny. Within an hour of getting home, she had to leave and report to the evacuation centre, which had just returned to recreation use that morning.

On September 5, the sky was once more filled with aircraft: helicopters with buckets scooped water from the pond on Ronny's golf course, dumping it on the fire's leading edge — only 4 kilometres away.

Wet Relief

Finally — on September 8 — rain fell on the city of Kelowna. Residents thought they were hallucinating. The precipitation buoyed the spirits of everyone, including the mayor, Walter Gray, who declared, "Clouds never looked so good." It was cooler too, so the evacuation alert affecting 4250 people was cancelled. Slimy white protective fire-retardant gel now covered their houses, but few complained. Some who had been evacuated twice didn't unpack for a while.

The fire continued to smoulder but away from any residences. Many out-of-town firefighting crews were able to go home the next day. On September 14, the longest provincial state of emergency was lifted. The military — the second largest deployment of armed forces after Afghanistan — could depart.

On September 21, six long weeks after the precipitating lightning bolt, the Kelowna fire was fully contained. More than 25,000 hectares had been destroyed. One victim said she couldn't walk in the forest behind her house anymore. "It feels like I shouldn't be there, like it wants to be left alone, to grow again."

British Columbia's costliest natural disaster — $550 million for firefighting, emergency services, and clean-up — prompted a full review. The report insisted new homes be fireproofed, high-risk areas be cleaned up, and firefighters better trained. BC was also advised again to return to controlled burns by the forest service, especially in high-risk interface zones.

By the start of summer 2004, the drought status continued, but Kelowna was looking its lush self again as it continued to rebuild. Two new wines from a burned-down winery — Glowing Amber Chardonnay and Fireman's Red — symbolized the phoenix rising from the ashes.

Epilogue

Weather is a complex and powerful force of nature that Canada has prided itself on coping with successfully throughout its history. In the last decade, though, the weather has increasingly challenged Canadians' ability to cope with, never mind control, it.

Weather catastrophes have prompted speculation about the links with global warming and the mysterious El Niño. Is the weather really getting worse? Is it just that the dramatic images of weather disasters make for "good TV," so we're hearing more about it? Or perhaps people have become less willing or prepared to deal with the elements?

Regardless, the fact is that half of all Canadian disasters have been caused by extreme weather. Although there's not much a person can do about the weather, Canadians must take some responsibility for the country's weather-related catastrophes. Urbanization influences the climate. Development changes not just the landscape, but also the environment, magnifying the impact of fires, floods, and power failures. Canadians living close to forests, or in drought or flood zones learn the risks, although sometimes only after devastating experiences.

The economic fallout of these disasters has intensified the worries of governments, insurance companies, and utility companies. The result? Canadians have developed better ways of predicting, curtailing, or at least coping with weather. Alberta is experimenting with hail suppression. Manitoba has its Floodway. Ice-prone Quebec now has stronger utility poles. The Prairies have adapted farming techniques, and BC will be adopting stronger fire-prevention strategies. Improved (or more sophisticated) weather forecasting will continue to be critical across the country.

And while wild weather can destroy communities, it can bring them together. Emergency workers such as police, firefighters, EMS, and the military can always be counted on. But everyday citizens have also emerged as heroes — from a gale-sniffer to a snowmobiler to someone's next-door neighbour. As long as the weather continues to wreak destruction, Canadians will continue to find ways to come together and diminish its blows.

Bibliography

Abley, Mark. *The Ice Storm: An Historic Record in Photographs of January 1998.* Toronto: McClelland & Stewart, 1998.

Abley, Mark. *Stories from the Ice Storm.* Toronto: McClelland & Stewart, 1999.

Anderson, Charles. *Wildfire: British Columbia Burns.* Vancouver: Greystone Books, 2003.

Benedict, Michael. *In the Face of Disaster: True Stories of Canadian Heroism from the Archives of Maclean's.* Toronto: Viking, 2000.

Braithwaite, Max. *The Hungry Thirties: 1930/40.* Toronto: Natural Science of Canada Ltd., 1977.

Broadfoot, Barry. *Next-Year Country: Voices of the Prairie People.* Toronto: McClelland & Stewart, 1988.

Broadfoot, Barry. *Ten Lost Years, 1929–1939: Memories of the Canadians Who Survived the Depression.* Toronto: McClelland & Stewart, 1973.

Bibliography

Brown, April Crawford. *Okanagan Mountain Fire.* Kelowna: Tiger Marketing, 2003.

Bumsted, J. M. *The Manitoba Flood of 1950: An Illustrated History.* Winnipeg: Watson and Dwyer Publishers, 1993.

Freake, Ross and Don Plant. *Firestorm: The Summer B.C. Burned.* Toronto: McClelland & Stewart, 2003.

Friesen, Gerald. *The Canadian Prairies: A History.* Toronto: University of Toronto Press, 1984.

Kennedy, Betty. *Hurricane Hazel.* Toronto: Macmillan of Canada, 1979.

Lingard, Mont. *The Newfie Bullet: The Story of Passenger Train Service in Newfoundland.* Grand Falls-Windsor: Mont Lingard Publishing, 2000.

Lingard, Mont. *Next Stop: Wreckhouse.* Grand Falls-Windsor: Mont Lingard Publishing, 1997.

Maher, Stephen. *Hurricane Juan: The Story of a Storm.* Halifax: Nimbus Publishing, 2003.

Phillips, David, *Blame It on the Weather: Strange Canadian Weather Facts.* Toronto: Key Porter Books, 1998.

Rossi, Erno. *White Death: The Blizzard of '77.* Port Colbourne: 77 Publishing, 1999.

Thomson, Tom. *Faces of the Flood.* Toronto: Stoddart, 1997.

Wheaton, Elaine. *But It's a Dry Cold: Weathering the Canadian Prairies.* Calgary: Fifth House, 1998.

Winnipeg Free Press. *A Red Sea Rising: The Flood of the Century.* Winnipeg: Winnipeg Free Press, 1997.

Acknowledgments

The stories of weather in Canada have been collected in many ways: newspaper accounts, diaries, technical books, and folklore. Because of their impact on so many people, some recent disasters have even spawned commemorative books to capture the timeline, stories, quotes, and photographs. *Wildfire, Okanagan Mountain Fire, A Red Sea Rising, Hurricane Juan: The Story of a Storm*, as well as *The Ice Storm, Stories from the Ice Storm*, and *White Death: The Blizzard of '77* each collected the memories and scenes of those amazing events in intimate and immediate detail. Thanks to these and Betty Kennedy's book on Hurricane Hazel and Barry Broadfoot's oral histories of the prairie people in the 1930s, a great variety of stories survive from the events.

This book is in debt to the books in the bibliography, as well as to a variety of expert sources who have spent a great deal of time studying these extreme weather events and/or who were there to witness Canada's weather first-hand. Thanks go out to Gloria Trimble, Environment Canada; Pat McCarthy, Prairie Storm Prediction Centre; Stuart Porter, Newfoundland Weather Centre; Bruce Whiffen and Gerard Morin, Atlantic Climate Centre; Brian McConkey, Agriculture and Agri-Food Canada; and Jim Renick, Alberta Severe Weather Management Society. Just as important are the people who took the time to share their personal experiences of these weather events. Those not already mentioned in the stories include: Bill Ackhurst, Phyllis Baird, Clayton Billard, Daniel Desroches, Dleap Hall, Jill Huffman, Andrea Marantz, and Mandy Ryan. Thank you all.

Photo Credits

Cover: Canadian Press (Jacques Boissinot); Canadian Press: pages 19 (Robert Galbraith), 92 (Winnipeg Free Press / Joe Bryksa), 102 (Halifax Chronicle Herald / Tim Krochak).

About the Author

Joan Dixon has lived in many parts of Canada and is personally acquainted with windstorms, firestorms, ice storms, hail, and blizzards. She considers herself lucky for never having experienced a hurricane or a flood. She and her family chose their current home in the foothills of Alberta for its topography and rarely boring weather: clear blue skies, chinooks ... and the possibility of snow all year round!

Joan holds a Master's degree in Canadian Studies, which is why she writes about amazing Canadian people and events. She is the author of two other books in the Amazing Stories series: *Trailblazing Sports Heroes* and *Roberta Bondar*.

OTHER AMAZING STORIES

ISBN	Title	ISBN	Title
1-55153-959-4	A War Bride's Story	1-55153-951-9	Ontario Murders
1-55153-794-X	Calgary Flames	1-55153-790-7	Ottawa Senators
1-55153-947-0	Canada's Rumrunners	1-55153-960-8	Ottawa Titans
1-55153-966-7	Canadian Spies	1-55153-945-4	Pierre Elliot Trudeau
1-55153-795-8	D-Day	1-55153-981-0	Rattenbury
1-55153-972-1	David Thompson	1-55153-991-8	Rebel Women
1-55153-982-9	Dinosaur Hunters	1-55153-995-0	Rescue Dogs
1-55153-970-5	Early Voyageurs	1-55153-985-3	Riding on the Wild Side
1-55153-798-2	Edmonton Oilers	1-55153-974-8	Risk Takers and Innovators
1-55153-968-3	Edwin Alonzo Boyd	1-55153-956-X	Robert Service
1-55153-996-9	Emily Carr	1-55153-799-0	Roberta Bondar
1-55153-961-6	Étienne Brûlé	1-55153-997-7	Sam Steele
1-55153-791-5	Extraordinary Accounts	1-55153-954-3	Snowmobile Adventures
	of Native Life on	1-55153-971-3	Stolen Horses
	the West Coast	1-55153-952-7	Strange Events
1-55153-992-6	Ghost Town Stories II	1-55153-783-4	Strange Events and More
1-55153-984-5	Ghost Town Stories III	1-55153-986-1	Tales from the West Coast
1-55153-993-4	Ghost Town Stories	1-55153-978-0	The Avro Arrow Story
1-55153-973-X	Great Canadian	1-55153-943-8	The Black Donnellys
	Love Stories	1-55153-942-X	The Halifax Explosion
1-55153-777-X	Great Cat Stories	1-55153-994-2	The Heart of a Horse
1-55153-946-2	Great Dog Stories	1-55153-944-6	The Life of a Loyalist
1-55153-773-7	Great Military Leaders	1-55153-787-7	The Mad Trapper
1-55153-785-0	Grey Owl	1-55153-789-3	The Mounties
1-55153-958-6	Hudson's Bay Company	1-55153-948-9	The War of 1812 Against
	Adventures		the States
1-55153-969-1	Klondike Joe Boyle	1-55153-788-5	Toronto Maple Leafs
1-55153-980-2	Legendary Show Jumpers	1-55153-976-4	Trailblazing
1-55153-775-3	Lucy Maud Montgomery		Sports Heroes
1-55153-967-5	Marie Anne Lagimodière	1-55153-977-2	Unsung Heroes of the
1-55153-964-0	Marilyn Bell		Royal Canadian Air Force
1-55153-999-3	Mary Schäffer	1-55153-792-3	Vancouver Canucks
1-55153-953-5	Moe Norman	1-55153-989-6	Vancouver's
1-55153-965-9	Native Chiefs and		Old-Time Scoundrels
	Famous Métis	1-55153-990-X	West Coast Adventures
1-55153-962-4	Niagara Daredevils	1-55153-987-X	Wilderness Tales
1-55153-793-1	Norman Bethune	1-55153-873-3	Women Explorers

These titles are available wherever you buy books. If you have trouble finding the book you want, call the Altitude order desk at **1-800-957-6888**, e-mail your request to: **orderdesk@altitudepublishing.com** or visit our Web site at **www.amazingstories.ca**

New AMAZING STORIES titles are published every month.